NOLA FOURNIER AND JANE FOURNIER

IN SHEEP'S CLOTHING

NOLA FOURNIER AND JANE FOURNIER

IN SHEEP'S CLOTHING

A HANDSPINNER'S GUIDE TO WOOL

INTERWEAVE PRESS

Cover Design, Michael Signorella, Signorella Graphic Arts
Interior Design, Marc McCoy Owens
Photography, Joe Coca unless otherwise specified
Illustration, Susan Strawn
Production, Marc McCoy Owens
Back cover photos, Diana McBride and Ron McNeely

Interweave Press, Inc.
201 East Fourth Street
Loveland, Colorado 80537 USA
www.interweave.com

Printed in the United States of America

The Library of Congress has cataloged the hardcover edition as follows:

Fournier, Nola, 1935–
    In sheep's clothing : a handspinners guide to wool / Nola Fournier and Jane Fournier.
        p.   cm.
    Includes bibliographical references and index.
    ISBN 1-883010-11-X
    1. Wool.   2. Sheep breeds.   I. Fournier, Jane, 1955–.   II. Title.
TS1547.F68   1995
    677'.31—dc20   95-23425
                                                                      CIP

ISBN 1-931499-38-1 (Pbk)

10 9 8 7 6 5 4 3 2

ACKNOWLEDGMENTS

The material for this book comes from many diverse sources and it would not have been possible to assemble it without the help and involvement of enthusiastic hand-spinners, wool growers, and sheep breeders from several countries. We thank you all.

We are especially grateful to Bruce Tinnock, Department of Wool Science, Lincoln University, Canterbury, New Zealand, for his unfailing willingness to help us steer an accurate course through the technical information. Lyn Finch, Elaine Soanes, and Deb Robson we thank for their advice and for sharing their knowledge. We would like to thank our Auntie Betty, Charlene Blincoe, Francie Dulieu, Ronelle Hyde, Shonagh Love, Pat Old, Judith Ryan, and Philippa Vine who spun yarns and made samples and finished pieces to support the text. We thank Alistair McCubbin for his graphics and IS support, and Patty White for her help in procuring fleece samples. We especially wish to thank Bill Fournier and Daniel Ellison for their enduring logistics and moral support.

For handspinners

TABLE OF CONTENTS

GETTING STARTED

A far greater range of fleeces is available to handspinners than most ever think of using—so often we limit ourselves to just a few breeds and a narrow range of fleece properties. The information in this book makes it easier to use more of the extensive range of wool available and suggests new ways to use familiar fleeces. Sensitivity to the properties of a fleece and an understanding of how those properties can be interpreted through the process of yarn production will enable you to make the very most of your creative ideas, raw materials, and skills.

A wealth of information related to handspinning can be found in the wool industry and in the literature of history, science, and agriculture. We have gathered useful details from these scattered sources and focused them specifically on the needs and interests of handspinners and textile craft workers.

This book contains information about wool, fleece types, and the processes used in the production of wool yarns. It is not an instruction book on handspinning, although certain techniques are discussed briefly. Instead, the book seeks to foster an understanding of the consequences of fleece selection and the various elements of yarn production that follow. There are few right and wrong ways of doing things. The success or failure of a handspun yarn or garment depends solely on how well it fits its unique role. Understanding and experience, not rules, are the most valuable tools for designing yarn. We hope to increase your understanding and to further your explorations in the exciting field of designing yarn.

Chapter 1 tells about wool and its important properties. We have included technical detail only where we felt it was essential.

In Chapters 2, 3, 4, and 5, we discuss specific kinds of sheep in terms of their fleece. The information is organized according to wool type and breed name. You may not have access to all of these wools, but we hope that you will find the information interesting. The breed names are of secondary importance; it is the type of wool that is in your hands that matters. The breed descriptions are a means to the end of describing the range of wools that you could find in your hands.

We have endeavored to include most of the breeds available in the United States, New Zealand, Australia, and the United Kingdom. Photographs of as many wool types as we could gather will help you to identify the characteristics of the breeds and can be used to compare with your own fleeces.

Naturally colored fleeces present their own opportunities and challenges, whatever their fleece type. In Chapter 6 you'll learn in what ways colored fleece differs from white fleece and how to make the most of that natural coloring.

Chapter 7 will take you through the necessary steps for selecting the best fleece for the job at hand. A handy table of common wool faults and remedies is included. Sorting and storing your fleece are also considered.

Chapter 8 presents some ideas for blending wools, both in all-wool combinations and with other fibers. This is an extensive subject, and we have only touched on the possibilities. We hope to stimulate your interest and get you started on this fascinating topic.

The terms and techniques in Chapter 9 reflect our preferences and define our vocabulary. The aim in this chapter is to increase your awareness of how different processes affect wool and wool yarns. It contains directions for various methods of wool preparation, our favorite spinning technique, and some finishing processes. And finally, a glossary clarifies the differences in terminology used in different countries.

Throughout the book, samples, swatches, examples, and Quick Reference Guides illustrate some of the concepts and fleece types. They demonstrate how fleece may be used to best advantage and how the characteristics of a given fleece may be used to achieve specific results.

YARN DESIGN

Yarn design may be approached from several directions. You can start with a purpose, a fleece, or an idea for a fabric or yarn. By the time you have arrived at a successful end product, all design criteria for what to make and how to make it must have been considered. It is preferable to make all the necessary decisions regarding comfort, durability, visual impact, and any other qualities important to the project at the beginning of the process, but you can make one decision at a time as each subsequent step adds to your understanding of the fiber and yarn.

While fiber preparation and spinning methods can minimize some limitations of the fleece, you can expect the properties of the fleece to be reflected in the yarn that you spin. Selecting a fleece with the right properties is a big step toward attaining your goal.

We have grouped the breeds into four categories based entirely on a handspinner's point of view. Each country and sheep-related industry has a method for defining groups of sheep or wool with similar qualities. Our categories—fine wool, longwool, down-type wool, and other wools—conform to generally accepted types of fleece. We have assigned each breed to one of these categories, solely according to our evaluation of its characteristics for handspinning; information on genetics, meat production, and origin have been mentioned only briefly. Those features are important, too, but when fiber is your main concern, they are secondary. To the handspinner, a breed name is a convenient way of summing up a collection of fleece characteristics and information with one or two words. The words *strong Corriedale*, for example, convey basic information about approximate fiber diameter, crimp, staple length, and so forth.

Many of the fleeces that you come across may have a cloudy parentage at best, but this in no way diminishes their worth. Throughout the book, we encourage you to look beyond the breed name to the qualities of a fleece, and also to look ahead through yarn design and production to envision the effect that these qualities will have on your yarns. With this approach, it doesn't matter what kind of fleece you are facing; you will be able to make the most of its unique attributes.

After you have determined a fleece's properties, you can assess its strengths, weaknesses, and peculiarities. If you want to identify a breed or type of fleece for a particular purpose, you may prefer to start with the Quick Reference Guides. These give an overview of the breeds and their fleece characteristics. Then turn to the text descriptions of the breeds which look most promising. Skim through the preparation methods to see which seem appropriate and will enhance the end use. Finally, look at some of the examples made from that type of fleece.

Once you've read the book, you will be ready to make your own yarn samples, refine your technique, and proceed with confidence toward your goal.

1
ABOUT WOOL

The time, skill, love, and care invested in the creation of handspun textiles demand the use of the best raw materials available. One of the most important components of craftsmanship is a sound understanding of basic materials. Without this knowledge, the full potential of a medium cannot be realized. The potter selects his clay according to his needs, the woodworker his woods, and so it is with the handspinner.

Wool is one of the most versatile and varied fibers spinners have used throughout history. It has contributed to the comfort and survival of humanity for thousands of years. Although today it accounts for only 5 percent of the world's fiber consumption, it remains an important trading commodity. The earliest fragments of wool fabric, dated to 4000–3500 BC, were found in Egypt. A German archaeological site yielded a sample that has been dated to 1500 BC. Other fragments of rough, coarse, wool fabric have been dated to 1300–1000 BC. With good management and some luck, wool will continue to be a significant fiber for many thousands of years to come. Let's take a look at some of its qualities so that we may appreciate its role in history and in our hands.

A beautiful fleece in the hands of a sensitive and knowledgeable spinner will be transformed into a superb yarn. The same fleece may become a most inappropriate and disappointing yarn if its natural characteristics are ignored. Nonetheless, the best spinner in the world cannot produce wonderful yarn from poor or mediocre fleece.

WOOL STRUCTURE

Wool is an animal protein (keratin) fiber. The outer sheath, the cuticle, makes up about 10 percent of the fiber, and the inner portion, the cortex, about 90 percent. Magnification shows the fiber to be elliptical in cross section and reveals that a thin but tough protective membrane covers the cuticle itself, a single layer of cells overlapping at the edges to form scales that point towards the tip of the fiber. Long-wool fiber has long, thin scales with very little overlap, making it is smooth and lustrous. Fine-wool fiber, on the other hand, has an irregular surface which breaks up reflected light, giving it a nonlustrous but brighter appearance.

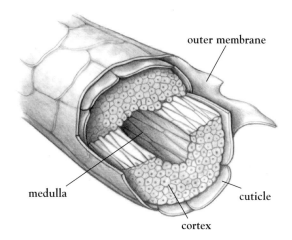

Cross section of wool fiber.

Within the cuticle lies the cortex, which is composed of long, spindle-shaped, closely packed cells which lie side by side. The cortex forms the greatest part of the fiber mass, and is responsible for the fiber's crimp and its behavior.

Inside the cortex, if present at all, is the medulla, a latticework of air-filled cells. Fine-wool fibers have little if any medulla whereas those dull, chalky, coarse fibers found in some wools may be as much as 90 percent medulla. The more medulla in a fiber, the less its strength and affinity for dyes.

GROWTH

Like all hair fibers—human hair included—wool grows out of the skin through follicles, narrow channels that protect the fiber as it forms and hardens. As it emerges through the skin, the fiber is lubricated by wax secreted by the sebaceous gland attached to the follicle. The fiber grows at

A growing wool fiber.

wool fiber

sweat duct

sebaceous gland

arrector muscle

sweat gland

different rates throughout the year according to the ratio of day to night and the amount of available feed.

Here is an experiment for you to try. Take a single wool fiber and hold it straight between your two hands. Close your eyes and move one of your little fingers (the little finger is usually more sensitive than the others) along the length of exposed fiber. Now move your finger back in the opposite direction. Does the fiber feel rougher in one direction than the other? If so, what you feel are the scales on the fiber surface. They are not visible to the naked eye but can usually be detected by this method. If you don't feel them, try again with a coarser fiber. The scales act to direct moisture and dirt away from the animal's body and they also play a major role in wool shrinkage.

WOOL CHARACTERISTICS

Wool is *strong* and *durable*. Although the individual fibers are the weakest of the natural fibers and much weaker than most synthetic fibers, wool nevertheless creates a sound and lasting fabric. Wool's remarkable springiness permits its fibers to be bent and folded repeatedly without breaking.

Wool is *elastic*. When dry, it can be stretched up to another third of its length—two thirds when the fibers are wet—and still return to its original size when released. The extension and recovery of the visible crimp of the fibers and similar stretching and recovery in the molecular structure of the wool fibers make this elasticity possible.

Wool is *warm*. A garment's warmth depends on several factors; the still air enclosed in the fabric, the still air enclosed between the fabric and the skin, and the heat generated when moisture is absorbed. The rough surface of the wool fiber, with its scales and crimp, provides ideal conditions for trapping air.

In addition, wool is *hygroscopic* (absorbs water readily); it gives off heat in return. In fact, wool can absorb up to one-third its weight in moisture without feeling damp. Under normal atmospheric conditions (65 percent relative humidity), about 14 percent of the fiber weight is water. If the moisture in the air increases, wool can continue to absorb another 20 percent of its dry weight before the wearer feels damp.

Wool is naturally *flame resistant*. Although it will ignite, it will not flare or continue to burn when the source of the flame is removed. Because it does not melt when burned, burning wool does not stick to skin as some synthetics do.

Wool fiber (like other animal fibers) moves more readily in one direction than the other. This phenomenon is called *differential friction effect* (DFE).

Try another experiment. Ask a friend to hold a single wool fiber extended between the thumb and index finger of each hand. With your index finger, stroke the fiber several times from left to right. Observe what if anything happens. Now, with the fiber still being held straight, stroke it from right to left. Can you see the fiber moving in one direction and not the other? When the fiber is rubbed, it travels towards its root end. The edges of the scales, which face toward the tip, catch against the adjacent surfaces making it easier for the fiber to ravel toward its root end.

This property can be an advantage or a disadvantage, depending on your point of view. Most of us have had some experience with a sweater inadvertently popped into the washing machine. It went in soft and fluffy at size 12 and emerged after its adventure with moisture, heat, and agitation as a blanket-style garment, now size 8. For the felter however, this is the property which makes their craft possible. DFE allows the fibers to become entangled and matted in a dense, compact configuration.

Movement of the fibers causes them to work toward their root ends, and the scales catch onto other nearby fibers so that they are unable to return to their original position when the agitation stops.

Pilling is the formation of tiny balls of fiber on the surface of a fabric. It occurs on areas of a garment that are subjected to abrasion, as where the sleeve rubs against the body. If you unravel a pill, you will find that the component fibers are relatively long. Rubbing eases the fibers out of the fabric and then rolls them into little balls. They are held on the fabric by longer fibers that have one end firmly anchored in the fabric and the other locked into the pill.

Wool pills can be easily removed by simply pulling them off the surface of a garment because the fiber length is limited. In synthetic fabrics, in which the fiber may be yards long, removing pills is more likely to damage the structure of the fabric. The more firmly the yarn is spun and the smoother the yarn, the less the likelihood of pilling.

Shrink-resistant wool is much less likely to pill than untreated wool. Several processes have been devised to add shrink resistance to wool fibers. The earliest industrial methods removed or reduced the projecting edges on the surface scales of the fiber; but they were found to cause significant fiber damage. Later methods include filling the cavities between the edge of the fiber and the tip of the scale with synthetic polymers, smoothing the fiber's rough, jagged surface.

Now that many people expect their woolen garments to be machine-washable, the International Wool Secretariat has determined a strict standard that can be used to measure the success of any shrink-resist process. Fiber or garments labeled *Superwash* must comply with this standard and can safely be machine washed. Recently, superwash wool top has become available to handspinners.

FINENESS CLASSIFICATION

The fineness of a fleece from a healthy sheep will tell you much about the softness and wearability of the wool. Generally, finer wool feels softer and wears less well compared with coarser wool.

Handspinners use two primary systems to describe the fineness of wool fibers: micron (μ) count and wool quality numbers. The difference between the two is that the micron count is a physical measurement whereas the quality number is a subjective assessment. It's helpful to be familiar with both sets of terminology

In New Zealand and Australia, wools are classified for fineness by micron count, which is an estimation of a fleece's average fiber diameter. A micron is one-millionth of a meter (or a thousandth of a millimeter). The lower the number, the finer the fleece.

In Britain and the United States, wool quality numbers are used. This system originated in the worsted industry in Bradford, England, and is sometimes referred to as the Bradford count or spinning count. It is based on the maximum number of skeins, each 560 yards long, that can be spun from

one pound of combed top. The higher the quality number, the finer the fleece—a 36s fleece is quite coarse and an 80s is very fine. Taking an 80s Merino as an example, this system implies that it is possible to spin 80 skeins, each 560 yards long, from one pound of prepared fleece. In reality, however, it is most unusual to spin to the maximum count of the wool.

To compare the two systems, an 80s Merino is roughly equivalent to a measurement of 18μ, whereas a 44/46s English Leicester measures about 36μ.

YARN TYPES

There are two main types of wool yarn, worsted and woolen. They are determined by

- the type of wool used to spin them;
- the preparation of that wool;
- the way the wool is spun.

Worsted yarns are spun from long fibers of similar length lying parallel to each other. They are usually made from longwools or fine wools, seldom from down-type wools. To ensure a parallel arrangement of the fibers and to remove any short fibers from within the staple, one of the combing methods must be used to prepare the wool for worsted spinning. As the yarn is spun, the drafting zone, where the fibers are attenuated immediately before they are twisted, is kept free of twist (in other words, the drafting of the fibers is completed before they are twisted) and the yarn is smoothed with the fingers to encourage protruding fibers to tuck themselves into the yarn.

Worsted wool is smooth, firm, and strong. The finished yarn has a characteristic sheen, especially when spun from a lustrous fleece.

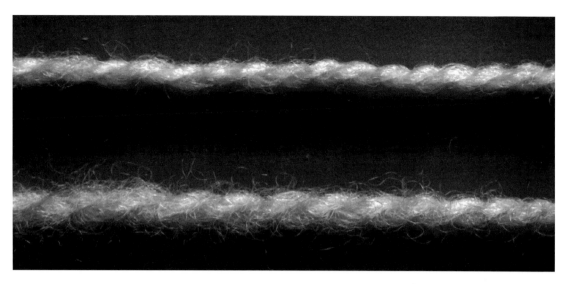

Top: *Worsted yarns are spun from long fibers of a similar length lying parallel to each other.*
Bottom: *Woolen yarns are spun from rolags, and the fibers are jumbled up in the yarn.*

Woolen yarns are spun from rolags. The wool is usually shorter than that used for worsted preparation. The short and long fibers of the fleece are carded together so that they are evenly prepared and organized into a manageable form. Because they are spun at right angles to their orientation in the rolag, the fibers will be jumbled up in the yarn, trapping plenty of air inside. The long-draw drafting method also retains as much air as possible between the fibers. Unlike worsted spinning, the drafting and the twisting take place at the same time when spinning a woolen yarn. Woolen yarns are fluffy, soft, warm, and lofty.

In addition to true worsted and woolen yarns, there are any number of intermediate combinations of preparation and spinning methods. Many handspinners spin what we call worsted-type or semi-worsted yarns. Flick-carded fiber, which does not truly remove all the short fibers, falls into this category. Drafting drum- or commercially-carded fleece draws out the fibers so that they are lying nearly parallel, and these preparation methods, too, can produce a worsted-type yarn which will be airier than a worsted yarn but smoother than a woolen yarn of the same fiber.

TYPES OF FLEECE

Sheep must surely produce a greater variety of body coverings than any other fiber-producing animal—almost like humans in fact! Our hair comes in a variety of color, length, and diameter (from coarse to fine); it can be straight, very curly, or anywhere between these two extremes. And so it is with sheep's fleeces, which vary in color, length, fiber diameter, and curl or crimp pattern.

All wool, whatever its characteristics, can be satisfactorily used for one purpose or another, but none can be satisfactorily used for *every* purpose. Sheep of different breeds offer different types of wool, and the knowledgeable fiberworker can make use of these differences to achieve particular objectives. First, however, it is necessary to be familiar with the variety of fleece types and their characteristics.

For the purposes of our discussion, there are three main types of wool from which a spinner may select:

◆ Fine wools
◆ Longwools (referred to in New Zealand as Crossbreds)
◆ Down wools

Look at the fine wools for *softness*, the longwools for *luster and strength*, and the down wools for *bulk without weight* and *maximum elasticity and resilience*.

Fine Wools

This group is characterized by fine average fiber diameters—50s to 90s (33μ to 17μ)—which generally means that fine wools feel softer than the other types. It provides great yarns for knitting and crochet, baby wear, and fine adult garments in which the soft handle or feel of the garment is of high importance. Fine wools blend well with other fine fibers—for example, silk, angora, or kid mohair—and produce woven fabric with superb draping qualities. Fine wools felt readily. They have traditionally been worsted spun, that is, spun into a smooth yarn from combed fiber, and are usually regarded as being "bright" in appearance—like sugar as opposed to household flour.

Longwools

Longwools have large average fiber diameters making them very hard-wearing but harsher to the touch than fine wools. Some of the finest of the longwools are suitable for heavier knitwear and outer garments such as jackets and heavy sweaters, but most are best suited for use in carpet-type yarns—that is, to make rugs, wall hangings, and upholstery. The stronger, very lustrous types of mohair will blend well with some longwools. Longwools can be worsted spun but are ideally suited to semiworsted spinning, which requires long, sound fiber (see page 170). Longwools are lustrous, and some have quite a silky handle.

Down Wools

Down wools are characterized by a very well developed spiral crimp that gives the wool exceptional elasticity. They have traditionally been used for medium- to lightweight knitwear yarns, hosiery, blankets, and tweeds. The spiraling form of the down-wool fiber confers crush resistance on woven fabric. Because these fleeces are usually shorter in staple than longwools and most fine wools, they are usually woolen spun. The springy nature of the fiber results in a full, round yarn. Its lusterless appearance may be described as "chalky".

2
FINE WOOLS

Rambouillet ewes carrying about eight months' of fleece growth.
Photograph by Jane Fournier.

The thread that ties all fine-wool breeds together is their relationship to the monarch of this group, the Merino. Apart from the pure Merino strains themselves, each of these breeds is the result of one or more other breeds' having been crossed with Merino. Most of these breeding efforts have been undertaken with the idea of creating a sheep better adapted to specific local conditions and with better meat characteristics than the Merino, while still capable of producing a heavy fleece of high-quality, fine wool. Many of these dual-purpose breeds have been remarkably successful, but still none can compete with Merino in growing the very finest fleeces.

Within the wool industry, the classification *fine* is often applied only to Meri-no-type wool. From the handspinner's point of view, all of the breeds collected in this group share similarities in handling and characteristics with each other and with Merino. Therefore, our definition of *fine wool* is practical, and it is broader.

Fine-wool sheep are generally medium-sized, with mature ewe weights between 110 and 140 pounds (49 and 64 kg), and have white faces and legs. Most of them tend to thrive on, but are not limited to, dry range grazing. The fleeces are medium to large, generally weighing between 9½ and 13 pounds (4.3 kg and 5.8 kg), and very dense, with average fineness ranging from 50s to 90s count (33μ to 17μ). Staple lengths range from 3½ to 5 inches (88 mm to 120 mm), which is short to medium compared with other breeds. Locks are generally well defined and rectangular with flat or slightly tapered tips. The crimp of most fine wools is very close (many crimps per inch/2.5 cm) and well developed, giving the wool excellent elasticity and loft. In appearance, it ranges from the precisely defined, V-shaped waves of Merino to the somewhat disorganized, three-dimensional waves of Targhee or Columbia. While fine wools are not generally noted for their luster, fleeces from breeds with Merino and longwool blood usually have a bright, reflective quality.

The wool from fine breeds is used commercially to make high-quality worsted and woolen fabrics, knitwear, and handknitting yarns. Handspinners have discovered that the finer fleeces from this group of breeds are soft enough for making next-to-the-skin wear and baby garments. The remainder are suitable for making lively yet soft, gently draping fabrics, either knitted or woven. Blended with other fibers, such as silk, cashmere, alpaca, or angora, carefully chosen fine fleeces can add bounce and elasticity to luxurious yarns without sacrificing softness and handle.

Rambouillet lock and yarn samples. From top, yarn samples are: six-ply cable yarn spun from hand-carded roving; flick-carded tips blended with Bombyx silk on a drum carder and spun into two-ply yarn; two-ply yarn spun from drum-carded fleece.

Fine wools have two properties that necessitate extra care when washing them. First, the grease in fine wools is characteristically waxy and tenacious, requiring very hot water and plenty of detergent to remove it completely. The amount of wool grease is abundant as well, resulting in substantial weight loss during washing. Second, these fleeces have a great tendency to felt and so should be handled carefully and as little as possible while wet.

Placing fleece in an open mesh bag for washing allows the suds to work their way in and the dirt to work its way out. For the finest fleeces, such as Merino, Rambouillet, Polwarth, comeback-type, and Targhee, washing an entire fleece at once does not remove all the grease. These very soft, fine wools are more satisfactorily cleansed in small portions to ensure thorough penetration of the washing agent and thorough rinsing.

For superfine fleece (any fleece with a fineness of 80s (18μ) or finer), the following method has proved to be very satisfactory. Have ready three bowls of really hot

This plaid fabric was woven from Targhee singles. The sample on the left has been brushed to emphasize its softness.

This knitted sample was a simple two-ply spun from drum-carded batts of Targhee.

This swatch was knit from four-ply yarn spun from drum-carded fleece with a long supported draw.

water (wear rubber gloves if necessary). One should contain plenty of detergent, and the others should be clear water for rinsing. You'll wash a small bundle of staples, about the size of a broom handle, at a time. Grasp the bundle of staples at about the midsection and immerse it in the detergent. With your free hand work the liquid into the tips, keeping the staples under water. Work liquid into the butt end and wiggle the staples around a bit. Rinse the bundle in the first bowl of clean water and then in the second bowl. Place the clean bundle on a towel.

Repeat until you have washed enough wool for your immediate needs and your towel is covered with neat rows of bundles. Roll up the towel and squeeze out any excess moisture. Lay the towel flat; the small bundles of fleece will dry very quickly. This may sound rather fiddly, but you can wash enough fleece to give you many hours' spinning pleasure in only fifteen to twenty minutes.

The plastic mesh bags used to pack fruit and vegetables make great containers for washing larger quantities of fleece. They can hold the staples in a single row and can be easily handled without disturbing the alignment of the fiber. Use the same general procedure as was described for washing the small bundles—plenty of detergent and two rinses—but let the fleece lie in the suds until the water is comfortably cooled down. Handle the bags by their ends. If you have several bags, you can put them in the washing machine on the spin-only cycle to remove the surplus water.

Fleece at the stronger end of the fine-wool range can be safely washed in larger quantities—say, a pound or two (500 g to 1 kg) at a time. Use mesh bags and plenty of detergent, and rinse thoroughly. Spin out the excess water.

When drying fleece, it's best to arrange the fiber so that air can circulate on all sides. You may leave the fleece in the bags for drying and hang the bags by their corners from a clothesline. A net sweater dryer is also handy for holding wool as it dries.

PREPARATION

Wool combs and flick carders are suitable tools for preparing fine wools. The wool combs remove all the short ends, if this is important for your yarn. The weathered tips of superfine fleece should almost always be pulled off before preparation; otherwise, they may break off and form dense clumps of short tangled fibers called neps. This may not be necessary if the sheep

QUICK REFERENCE GUIDE TO FINE WOOLS					
Breed	**Softness**	**Elasticity & Loft**	**Staple Length**	**Luster**	**Felting Properties**
Bond	◆◆◆▾	◆◆◆▾	◆◆◆▾	◆◆◆	◆◆◆◆
CVM	◆◆◆◆	◆◆◆◆	◆◆▾	◆◆	◆◆◆▾
Columbia	◆◆◆▾	◆◆◆◆	◆◆◆	◆◆	◆◆◆▾
Comeback	◆◆◆◆	◆◆◆◆	◆◆◆	◆◆	◆◆◆◆▾
Cormo	◆◆◆◆	◆◆◆◆	◆◆◆	◆◆	◆◆◆◆▾
Corriedale	◆◆◆▾	◆◆◆	◆◆◆	◆◆◆	◆◆◆◆
Debouillet	◆◆◆◆◆	◆◆◆◆	◆◆◆	◆◆	◆◆◆◆◆
Dormer	◆◆◆◆	◆◆◆◆	◆◆▾	◆◆	◆◆◆◆
Merino	◆◆◆◆◆	◆◆◆◆	◆◆▾	◆◆▾	◆◆◆◆◆
NZ Halfbred	◆◆◆▾	◆◆◆▾	◆◆◆	◆◆◆	◆◆◆◆
Panama	◆◆◆▾	◆◆◆◆	◆◆◆	◆◆	◆◆◆▾
Polwarth	◆◆◆◆	◆◆◆◆	◆◆◆	◆◆▾	◆◆◆◆
Polypay	◆◆◆▾	◆◆◆◆	◆◆▾	◆◆	◆◆◆◆
Rambouillet	◆◆◆◆◆	◆◆◆◆	◆◆▾	◆◆	◆◆◆◆▾
Romeldale	◆◆◆◆	◆◆◆◆	◆◆◆	◆◆	◆◆◆▾
Targhee	◆◆◆◆	◆◆◆◆	◆◆◆	◆◆	◆◆◆◆
Zenith	◆◆◆◆	◆◆◆◆	◆◆◆	◆◆	◆◆◆◆

Five diamonds indicate the maximum amount of the quality listed.

Knitted lace of fine two-ply Merino spun from flick-carded locks.

have worn coats, which protect the wool from weathering.

If you decide to have your fleece custom-carded, be sure that the carding company has equipment than can satisfactorily handle fine fibers. The same applies to the use of hand carders: fine card clothing such as that found on "cotton" carders will yield higher-quality rolled batts of carded fiber, called rolags, from fine wool than will coarse card clothing, such as that found on "wool" carders. Fleece carded with inadequate equipment will contain neps, which can be very hard to eliminate. Cotton carders are effective and efficient tools for woolen yarn preparation and for blending fine wool with other fine fibers.

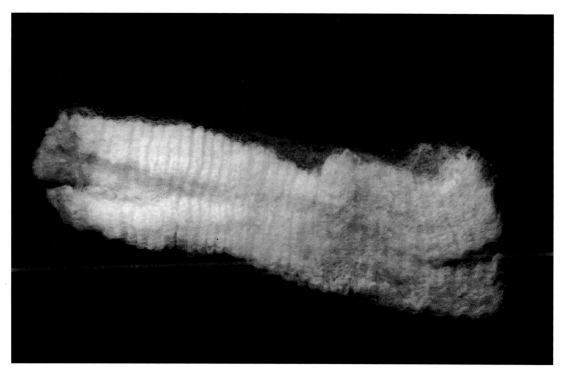

Bond sheep originated in Australia in 1909 from the mating of Saxon/Peppin Merino ewes to Lincoln rams; the offspring were selected for their ability to tolerate heavy rainfall. This breed was once known as the Commercial Corriedale because it produces a heavy fleece closer to the Merino than the traditional Corriedale, lying somewhere between Corriedale and Polwarth. Bond sheep have white faces and ears, and may have black mottles on their noses. Their legs are white with light-colored hooves, and both sexes are polled (hornless). The wool is soft with a regular and well-defined crimp. The staples are firm and usually rectangular, with fairly flat tips. Commercial uses for the wool include blankets, knitting wools, and military uniforms.

Fleece weight: 12–16 pounds (5.5 kg–7.5 kg)
Fiber diameter: 56s–60s (28μ–23μ)
Staple length: 6–7 inches (150 mm–180 mm)
Found in: Australia

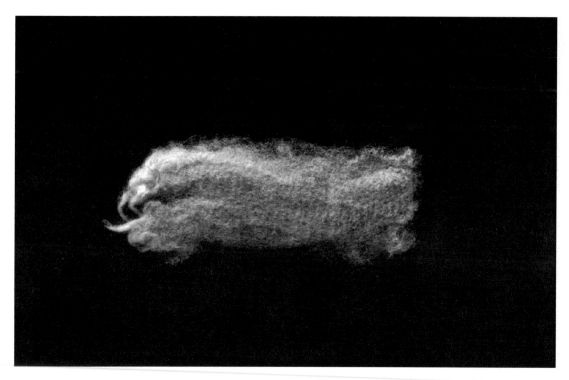

The California Variegated Mutant (CVM) originated in the United States as a naturally colored variant of the Romeldale; it shares many of the Romeldale characteristics (see page 44). The CVM is a dual-purpose breed, and selection has emphasized both fleece quality and lambing performance.

The color patterns of CVM vary widely. Many of these sheep have a characteristic striped "badger" face. Wool colors include white, gray, black, and brown, usually with several shades in a single fleece.

CVM locks have blunt or slightly tapered tips. The crimp is well developed, giving the wool a full, slightly crisp hand. Handspinners find that the wealth of shades in each fleece opens up many possibilities for the creative use of natural colors.

Fleece weight: 10–15 pounds (4.5 kg–7 kg)
Fiber diameter: 60s–64s (25μ–21μ)
Staple length: 3–4½ inches (75 mm–115 mm)
Found in: United States

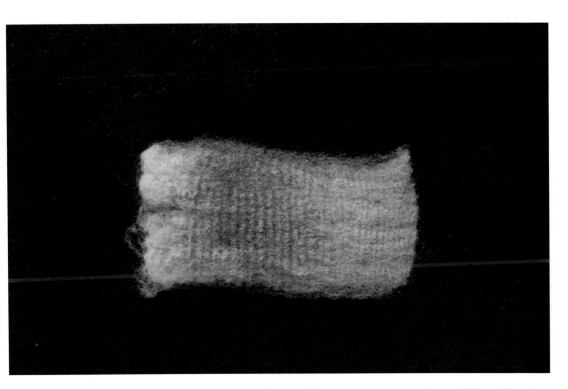

The Columbia was the first sheep breed to be developed in the United States. Breeding and selection started in 1912, based on a foundation of Lincoln rams crossed with Rambouillet ewes. The Columbia is larger than similar crossbred sheep. Animals have been selected solely to produce crossbred market lambs and a heavy, good-quality fleece.

Columbias have open, white faces, and they have wool on their legs. They are hardy sheep with good herding instincts and are particularly well adapted to the western rangelands of the United States.

The wool has excellent loft and body, a slightly crisp hand, and little luster. The staples are blocky in shape and have an indistinct but well-developed crimp. It is suitable for all preparation and spinning methods and is an excellent choice for a wide range of knitted and woven garments.

Fleece weight: 10–15 lbs (4.5 kg–7 kg)
Fiber diameter: 50s–60s (31μ–24μ)
Staple length: 3½–5 inches (90 mm–130 mm)
Found in: United States, Canada

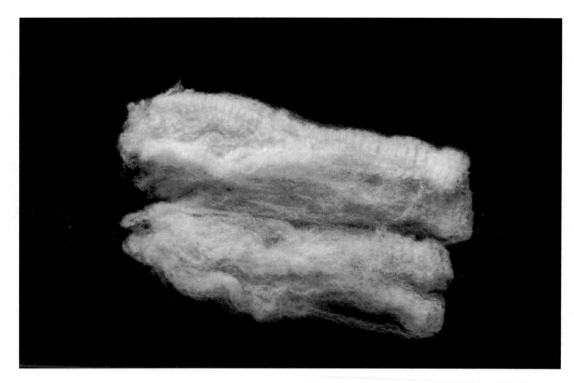

This Australian sheep type has developed by crossing large-framed Merino rams on a British longwool breed or a breed derived from a British longwool/Merino cross. Breeders were looking for a sheep producing a fine, heavy fleece, that would be less prone to parasites and better thriving than the Merino in higher rainfall areas. A Comeback Breeders Association was formed in 1976.

The term *comeback* refers to breeding back towards the merino and may be used to describe any fleece that is 70% to 90% Merino. Although there is a breeders association, the comeback is a type of sheep rather then a distinct breed. The sheep are similar in appearance to strong-wool Merinos but the face is more open and there are no neck folds.

The fleece is fine and soft and is used for woollen and worsted fabrics, hand knitting yarns, and felts.

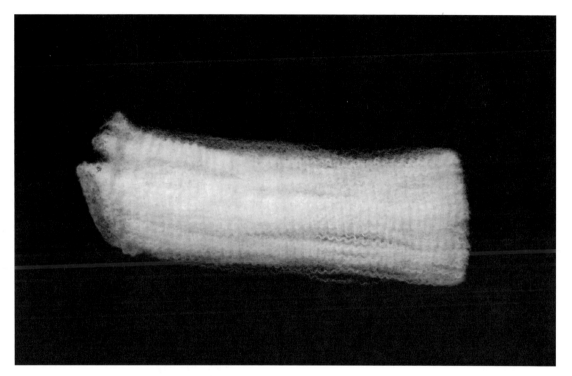

This Australian breed was derived from a crossing of Corriedale rams with Saxon Merino ewes; the offspring were rigorously selected for fine fiber diameter, good growth rates, and high clean-fleece weights. The Cormo withstands wet and cold conditions better than the Merino. Attention to fiber diameter in the wool ensures a finer fleece than Polwarth and more consistency in fiber diameter than comeback-type fleece.

Cormos have clean, white faces and legs, and soft pink skin with some mottles on their noses. The fine soft fleece has firm rectangular staples and a distinct, regular crimp. The wool is used to make fashion fabrics.

Fleece weight: 9–12 pounds (4 kg–5.5 kg)
Fiber diameter: 58s–64s (23μ–21μ)
Staple length: 4–5 inches (100 mm–130 mm)
Found in: Australia, United States

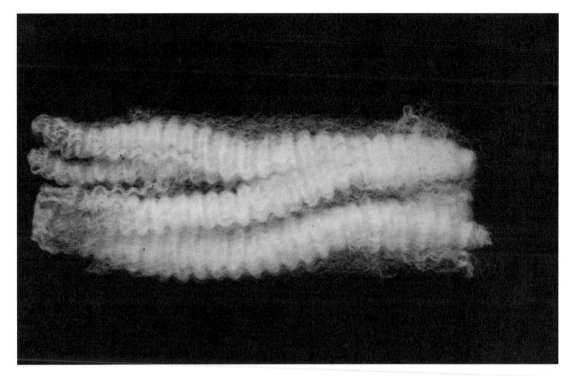

The Corriedale was the result of New Zealand's first breeding program, begun in 1868. Crossing British longwool rams (mainly Lincoln and English Leicester) with Merino ewes and then interbreeding the offspring produced a hardy animal adapted to a wide range of conditions and capable of providing both good meat and a heavy fleece.

These medium-sized sheep have white faces and legs, and black noses. They sometimes have wool on their faces, and they have very woolly polls, called topknots.

Corriedale fleece is fine, reasonably soft, and well crimped. The staples are firm and usually rectangular, with fairly flat tips. Corriedale is used commercially for worsteds and light tweeds, blankets, knitting wools, and hosiery.

Fleece weight: 10–13 pounds (4.5 kg–6 kg)
Fiber diameter: 50s–58s (33µ–26µ)
Staple length: 3–5 inches (75 mm–125 mm)
Found in: Australia, New Zealand, United States, South Africa, Argentina, Chile, China, United Kingdom

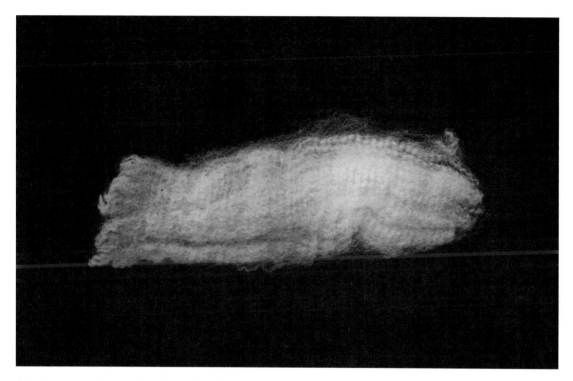

This breed was developed in the United States, beginning in 1920 with a cross of Delaine-Merinos and Rambouillets. Debouillets are hardy animals with excellent herding instincts, and they are particularly well adapted to the ranges of the southwestern United States where the breed originated.

Debouillets are medium-sized, and have white faces and legs. For Merino-type sheep, they are relatively smooth-bodied, and they have some wool on their legs. The rams may have horns, but there are also polled strains.

As you might expect from the breed's parentage, Debouillet fleece is fine and has excellent crimp and loft. The wool tends to be slightly longer than that of either Delaine-Merino or Rambouillet. Softness and drape make this a good choice for making baby wear, next-to-the-skin fabrics, or any other project suitable for Merino.

Fleece weight: 9–14 pounds (4 kg–6.5 kg)
Fiber diameter: 62s–80s (24μ–19μ)
Staple length: 3–5 inches (75 mm–125 mm)
Found in: United States

Developed in Australia in 1972, The Dormer was developed from crosses between multiple-birth Merino rams and polled and horned Dorset ewes. The male progeny of the original cross were crossed with Merino ewes to produce a 1/4 Dorset and 3/4 Merino sheep with a comeback-type fleece. It is a dual-purpose breed with an extended breeding season. Dormers have white faces, ears, and legs, and they resemble strong-wool Merinos.

Fleece weight: 9–11 pounds (4 kg–5 kg)
Fiber diameter: 58s–60s (25μ–23μ)
Staple length: $3\frac{1}{2}$–4 inches (90 mm–100 mm)
Found in: Australia

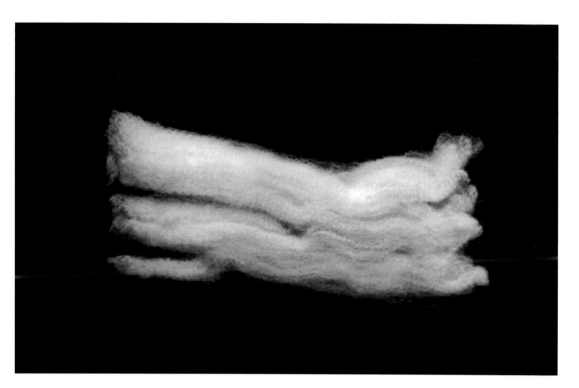

The pride of the flock, the Merino is the oldest and most numerous established breed in the world. The breed is believed to have come from North Africa, but it was after the Moors introduced them into Spain that these sheep became so highly prized and valuable.

The name *Merino* was firmly attached to this type of sheep in the late seventeenth century, but few animals left Spain until the decline of the Spanish Empire in the eighteenth century. Before then, the exportation of Spanish Merinos was a criminal offence commanding the death penalty! Gradually the breed became established elsewhere in Europe, and Merinos were the first sheep in New Zealand.

Merinos are fine-boned, active animals, with white faces, pink skin, and long, thin legs. Most have characteristic deep folds of skin at the neck, but these are less evident in some strains than in others. The rams and some of the ewes are horned. Recently, a polled strain has been developed, as well as a high-fertility Booroola strain to increase lambing percentages.

The wool is the finest of all the breeds, has a very soft handle, and consequently usually commands the highest price. A Merino fleece has about 50,000,000 fibers compared to about 15,000,000 in a Romney fleece.

The yield of clean wool from a Merino fleece is low compared to that of other breeds because of its high grease content—as much as 25 to 45 percent of the total fleece weight. The firm staples are rectangular, with very well-defined crimp and flat tips. Commercially, the fleece is used for high-quality apparel. Handspinners find it valuable for baby wear, and fine next-to-the-skin adult garments.

Sharlea is the registered name for ultra-fine Merino wool marketed by the Sharlea Ultra Fine Society of Australia. The sheep are housed in special barns, and their diet is carefully controlled to ensure superior fleece.

The wool is renowned for its uniformity of fineness and crimp, freedom from vegetable matter, superior tensile strength, and no weathering on the tips. The wool is carefully measured for fineness and it must be no more than 17.5μ to be accepted as Sharlea.

Fleece weight: 7–13 pounds (3.5 kg–6 kg)
Fiber diameter: 60s–70s (24μ–18μ)
Staple length: 2½–4 inches (65 mm–100 mm)
Found in: Australia, France, New Zealand, South Africa, United States, other countries

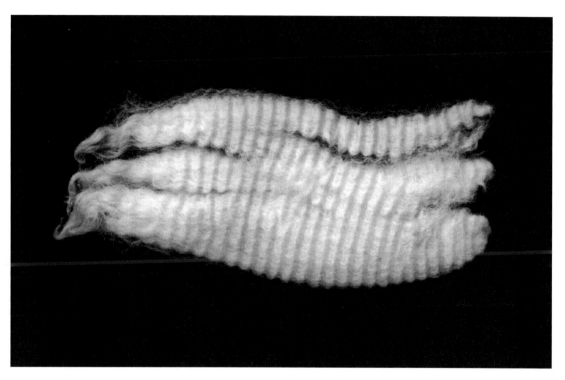

The New Zealand Halfbred was developed in the nineteenth century by crossing Leicester, Lincoln, or Romney rams with Merino ewes. These sheep had faster growth rates and better resistance to disease than the Merino. New Zealand Halfbreds are dual-purpose sheep, with the emphasis on wool production. To gain admittance to the breed registry, a Halfbred must be the offspring of a registered Merino and any long-wool breed. (Continued interbreeding of the offspring of the original crosses resulted in the Corriedale.)

New Zealand Halfbreds are medium-sized with white faces and pink noses. Their legs are white and are often covered with wool.

The staples are rectangular and firm with well-defined crimp. The tips are fairly flat in finer wools and slightly pointed in stronger fleece.

The wool has found much favor with overseas buyers, and is used for fine knitwear and fabric. Handspinners find it ideal for fine sweaters, soft durable fabrics, and blending with other fibers of medium fineness such as mohair and alpaca.

Fleece weight: 9–11 pounds (4 kg–5 kg)
Fiber diameter: 50s–58s (31μ–25μ)
Staple length: 3–4¹/₂ inches (75 mm–110 mm)
Found in: New Zealand

This breed was developed in the United States, starting in 1912 from a foundation of Rambouillet rams crossed with Lincoln ewes. After the initial cross, the offspring were interbred. The Panama breed is very similar to the Columbia, which was developed from an initial cross of Lincoln rams and Rambouillet ewes. Panamas are slightly smaller than Columbias because they were selected with more emphasis on meat production and less on size. They do well on the rangelands of the western United States, and they produce heavy fleeces.

Panamas are white faced and polled with some wool on the legs. The wool has very little luster and a well-developed but slightly disorganized crimp that results in very good loft and elasticity. The staples are blocky in shape wth very short tips. The wool can be used to produce a wide range of high-quality fabrics.

Fleece weight: About 13 pounds (6 kg)
Fiber diameter: 50s–58s (30μ–25μ)
Staple length: 3½–5 inches (90 mm–125 mm)
Found in: United States, Canada

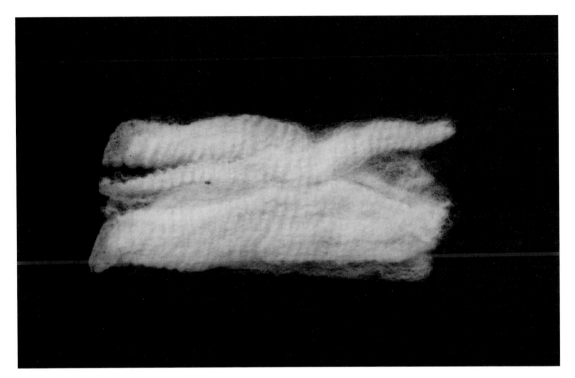

Polwarths were developed in Australia in 1880, when Lincoln × Merino ewes were bred back to Merino rams to produce a dual-purpose breed with an emphasis on wool production.

These sheep are clean-faced and pink-nosed with woolly topknots. Polled sheep are now more common than the original horned animals.

The fleece is white, bright, fine, and soft—second in softness only to that of the Merino. The staples are firm and rectangular with fairly flat tips and a well-defined, rounded crimp.

Fine woven and knitted fabrics made of Polwarth drape well. Yarn is best spun with a worsted or worsted-type technique for maximum durability; in patterned knitwear, the smooth yarn shows the pattern to best advantage. This wool is suitable for use in baby clothing and for blending with other fine fibers. Commercially, it is used to make worsted fabric, knitting yarns, and apparel.

Fleece weight: 9–11 pounds (4 kg–5 kg)
Fiber diameter: 58s–64s (26μ–21μ)
Staple length: 4–5½ inches (100 mm–140 mm)
Found in: Australia, New Zealand; small numbers in United Kingdom

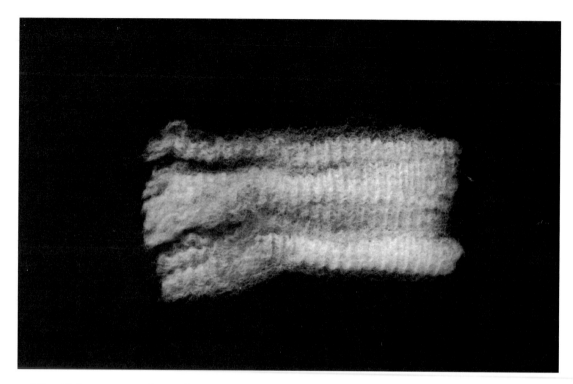

The Polypay is a relatively recent entry on the list of breeds in the United States. Development began in 1968 with initial crosses of Targhee × Dorset and Rambouillet × Finnsheep. The aims were a large early lamb crop, lambing more than once a year, rapid growth rate, and high meat yield.

Polypays are medium-sized, polled sheep with white faces. Because of the recent formation of this breed and its ongoing development, body type, size, and fleece characteristics are variable.

Polypay fleece is generally medium to fine with short, tapered tips and good loft. The crimp is usually well developed but can be wavy or disorganized. Some fleeces have a crisp handle whereas others are silky. Because of its unpredictability, Polypay fleeces are best selected by sample, in person, or from a known flock if specific qualities are needed. Choose them for making warm, softly draping fabrics, blankets, and sweaters.

Fleece weight: 9–11 pounds (4 kg–5 kg)
Fiber diameter: 56s–62s (28μ–22μ)
Staple length: 3–4 inches (75 mm–100 mm)
Found in: United States, Canada

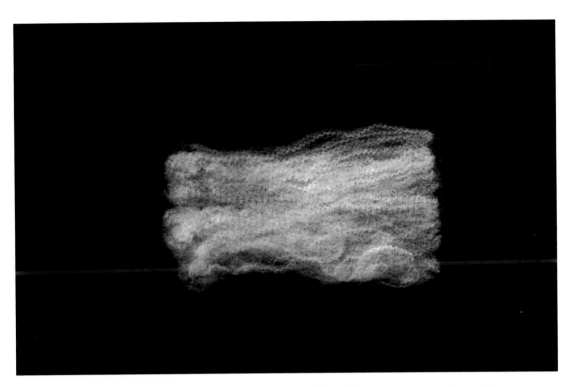

This breed takes its name from the estate of King Louis XVI at Rambouillet, France, where in 1786 a flock of pure Spanish Merinos was established. After careful selection and breeding with other Merino flocks, the Rambouillet breed became a distinct entity. They were introduced to the United States from the French royal flock, and they became the foundation of most of the United States' western range breeds.

Rambouillets are large, rugged, smooth-bodied, and moderately fast growing. Most rams have spiral horns, but there are also polled strains. They are gregarious as well as adaptable foragers, and they thrive in arid conditions. Although they have acceptable meat quality, Rambouillets are raised primarily for their high-quality fine wool.

The fleece is very soft and has a pronounced though slightly disorganized crimp, which gives it extremely good elasticity and excellent loft. The short staples are rectangular and have square, often dirty, tips.

Rambouillet wool can be used for baby wear and next-to-the-skin knitted or woven fabrics, as well as for blending with fine exotic fibers. While not as lustrous as Merino, it is more elastic and loftier. It is a good choice when these qualities are of paramount importance.

Fleece weight: 9–14 pounds (4 kg–6.5 kg)
Fiber diameter: 60s–80s (24μ–18μ)
Staple length: 2–4 inches (50 mm–100 mm)
Found in: France, United States

The Romeldale was developed in California in 1915 from an original cross of imported Romney rams and Rambouillet ewes. The result is a dual-purpose sheep that does well on rangeland.

Romeldales have open white faces; like Columbias, which they resemble, they are polled. In addition to acceptable meat yields, Romeldales produce heavy fleeces of fine wool with good staple length.

The wool has very little luster and blocky staples with very short, tapered tips. It has a pronounced crimp, which makes it ideal for making warm, soft, lightweight knitted and woven fabrics.

Fleece weight: 10–15 pounds (4.5 kg–7 kg)
Fiber diameter: 60s–64s (25μ–21μ)
Staple length: 3–4½ inches (75 mm–115 mm)
Found in: United States

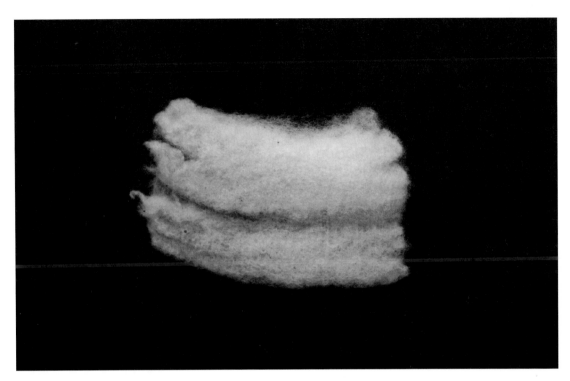

The Targhee was developed by the United States Department of Agriculture as a dual-purpose sheep adapted to the dry western rangelands. The foundation of the breed was a cross of Rambouillet rams and Corriedale × Lincoln/Rambouillet ewes. Targhees are raised both for crossbreeding with other meat breeds for market lamb production and for high-quality apparel wool.

Targhees are moderate-sized, polled sheep with open white faces.

The fleece is fine and dense with very good loft, indistinct but well-developed crimp, and short staple length. The staples are blocky in shape, with almost no luster.

The extraordinary loft and elasticity of Targhee make it particularly suitable for fine, light, knitted and woven fabrics with good shape retention and crease resistance. In blends with other short fibers, Targhee adds loft and elasticity.

Fleece weight: 10–14 pounds (4.5 kg–6.5 kg)
Fiber diameter: 58s–64s (27μ–22μ)
Staple length: 3–4¹/₂ inches (75 mm–110 mm)
Found in: United States, Canada

45

ZENITH

Like the Polwarth, the Zenith is another of the comeback-type sheep bred in Australia from Merino and Lincoln stock. It is a dual-purpose breed, similar in appearance to the Polwarth and Comeback.

Zeniths have clean, white faces and legs and large ears; they are polled. The fleece is used commercially in suitings and blankets.

Fleece weight: 10–12 pounds (4.5 kg–5.5 kg)
Fiber diameter: 58s–64s (25μ–21μ)
Staple length: 3½–5 inches (90 mm–125 mm)
Found in: Australia

3
LONGWOOLS AND CROSSBRED WOOLS

English Leicester ewe.
Photograph by Daniel Ellison.

This category includes a broad range of breeds, most of which originated from British sheep breeds. The fleeces in this group generally have a wavy crimp pattern and medium to long staple—from about 5 to 8½ inches (130 mm to 220 mm) with a few as long as 12 inches (300 mm). They range in fiber diameters from medium to coarse—48s to 36s (32µ to more than 40µ)—which makes them most suitable for making outerwear, upholstery, rugs, and carpets. The wool tends to be lustrous or semilustrous, except in the case of a naturally occurring mutation in Romney sheep that stimulates the growth of a hairy fleece that has heavily medullated fibers (each fiber has a large medulla) with little crimp and almost no luster.

Selecting the best long-wool or crossbred fleece for a project depends to a large extent on the amount of loft and durability that you require in the finished product. Although preparation and spinning method play important parts in making the most of loft, choice of fleece is the paramount factor. Lofty fleeces are generally more suitable for use in knitted sweaters and woven fabrics, in which warmth without excessive weight is the goal.

A yarn's capacity to wear well is related to both a coarse fiber diameter and a high degree of resilience in the fleece. Although wear resistance is important for any textile, it is particularly significant for upholstery and rug or carpet yarns. Crossbred or longwool type fleeces are eminently suitable for these uses.

47

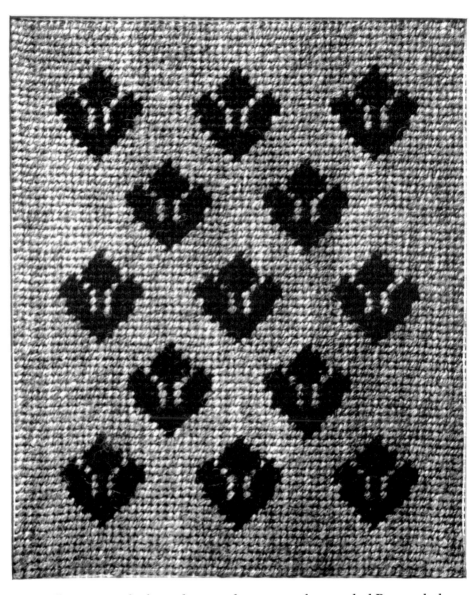

Needlepoint swatch of two-ply worsted yarns spun from combed Romney locks.

Finnish Landrace lock and yarn samples. Clockwise from upper left: singles spun from drum-carded fleece; two-ply spun from drum-carded fleece; three-ply spun from flick-carded locks; softly spun blend of Finnish Landrace and kid mohair; dark fleece blended with an equal part of kid mohair to make a designer yarn.

WASHING

Most long-wool and crossbred-type wools are moderately greasy and are easy to wash with little special attention. The lock structure can be easily preserved by washing the sorted fleece in a large mesh bag. Unless the fleece has been stored in the grease for a long time, the wool wax stays fluid and comes right out with hot water and detergent. On the whole, these fleeces have little tendency to felt; however, there are exceptions. Gotland and some of the other finer breeds in this group require a little extra care to ensure that they stay unmatted. Long-wool fleeces may compress during washing, so gently lift and turn the wet fleece occasionally to allow the air to circulate and encourage fast, even drying.

Hooked rug sample from finger-twisted locks of strong Romney fleece.

PREPARATION

All methods of fiber preparation are suitable for long-wool and crossbred breeds. Staple length and cleanliness, along with intended use, will help determine which method to use. Flick-carding is ideal for fast preparation of clean fleeces, whereas combing will take advantage of strength and enhance luster. Spend a little extra time to prepare very long staples for drum-carding by cleaning and separating clumped tip and butt ends with either your fingers or a flick carder. This will prevent fibers from tangling and jamming the machine. Hand-carding is recommended only for the shorter fleeces, as long staples may tangle during preparation and spinning.

Card-woven braid of English Leicester wool combed and spun with a short worsted draw.

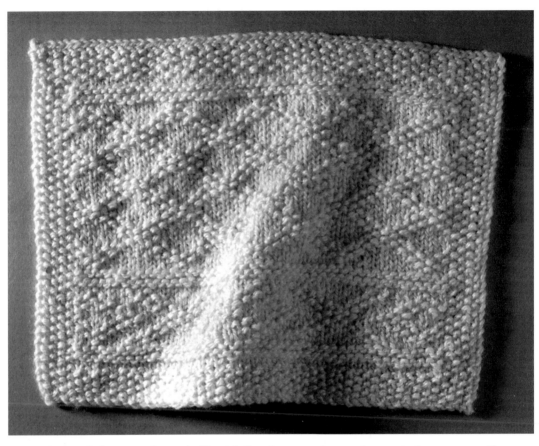

A smooth, lustrous three-ply Finnish Landrace wool yarn shows stitch patterns well.

Breed	Softness	Elasticity & Loft	Staple Length	Luster	Felting Properties
Blue-Faced Leicester	◆◆◆▾	◆◆▾	◆◆◆	◆◆◆	◆◆▾
Borderdale	◆◆◆	◆◆◆	◆◆◆	◆◆◆	◆◆◆▾
Border Leicester	◆▾	◆▾	◆◆◆◆	◆◆◆◆	◆◆
Carpetmaster	▾	▾	◆◆◆◆◆	▾	◆
Coopworth	◆◆	◆◆	◆◆◆▾	◆◆◆◆	◆◆◆
Cotswold	◆▾	◆▾	◆◆◆◆◆	◆◆◆◆▾	◆◆
Dartmoor	◆	◆	◆◆◆◆	◆◆◆◆	◆◆
Devon & Cornwall	◆	◆	◆◆◆◆◆	◆◆◆◆	◆◆
Drysdale	▾	▾	◆◆◆◆◆	▾	◆
Elliotdale	▾	▾	◆◆◆◆◆	▾	◆
English Leicester	◆▾	◆	◆◆◆◆◆	◆◆◆◆▾	◆◆▾
Finnish Landrace	◆◆◆▾	◆◆◆	◆◆◆	◆◆◆▾	◆◆◆▾
Gotland	◆◆◆	◆◆	◆◆▾	◆◆◆▾	◆◆◆◆
Gromark	◆◆◆	◆◆▾	◆◆◆	◆◆◆	◆◆◆▾
Lincoln	◆	◆	◆◆◆◆◆	◆◆◆◆◆	◆◆▾
Masham	◆◆▾	◆◆	◆◆◆◆◆	◆◆◆▾	◆◆▾
Mule	◆◆◆	◆◆▾	◆◆◆◆▾	◆◆◆▾	◆◆▾
Perendale	◆◆▾	◆◆◆▾	◆◆◆▾	◆◆▾	◆◆▾
Romney	◆◆▾	◆◆◆	◆◆◆▾	◆◆◆▾	◆◆◆▾
Teeswater	◆◆▾	◆◆	◆◆◆◆◆	◆◆◆◆◆	◆◆
Texel	◆◆◆	◆◆◆	◆◆◆	◆◆▾	◆◆▾
Tukidale	▾	▾	◆◆◆◆◆	▾	◆
Wensleydale	◆◆▾	◆◆	◆◆◆◆◆	◆◆◆◆◆	◆◆

Five diamonds indicate the maximum amount of the quality.

53

Sometimes known as the Hexam Leicester, this breed emerged in Britain about the turn of the century for the purpose of producing crossbred ewes from many of the hill breeds. It is one of the most prolific of the British breeds and is the sire of the Mule crossbred.

Blue-Faced Leicesters are polled, have broad Roman noses, and are free of wool on their white heads and legs. Their name comes from the dark blue skin which shows through the hair on their heads.

The fleece is relatively fine for a long-wool and semilustrous. The staples form long, narrow, curly locks. In part because it is so fine, Blue-Faced Leicester wool is also soft and silky. It is a good choice for making strong, smooth fabrics and yarns that drape well.

Fleece weight: 2½–4½ pounds (1 kg 2 kg)
Fiber diameter: 56s–60s (28μ–24μ)
Staple length: 3–6 inches (80 mm–150 mm)
Found in: United Kingdom, Canada, United States

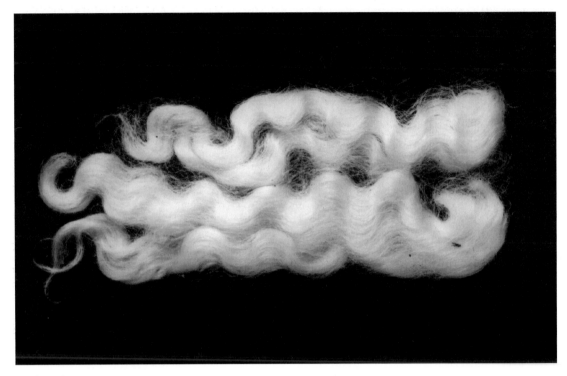

Border Leicesters are large, noble-looking sheep with clean heads and Roman noses. They have distinctive erect ears, and their legs are clean below the knee.

The breed is thought to have been developed in the late eighteenth century from English Leicester and Cheviot crosses, and it is named for the area where it evolved: the English borderlands between England and Scotland. Border Leicester ewes are highly fertile and make excellent mothers. The breed is often used to improve fertility in Romney and Corriedale flocks.

The fleece is long, lustrous, and curly, with clearly defined staples. These can be round or flat, and they frequently have corkscrew tips.

Border Leicester wool is suitable for use in upholstery fabric and coatings, and for blending with stronger types of mohair. A finer Border Leicester fleece with a silky handle can become great sweater yarn. Commercially, the wool is used for upholstery, dress fabrics, and handknitting wools.

Fleece weight: 10–13 pounds (4.5 kg–6 kg)
Fiber diameter: 36s–48s (40μ–37μ)
Staple length: 6–8 inches (150 mm–200 mm)
Found in: Northern England and Scottish Lowlands, Australia, New Zealand, South Africa, North and South America

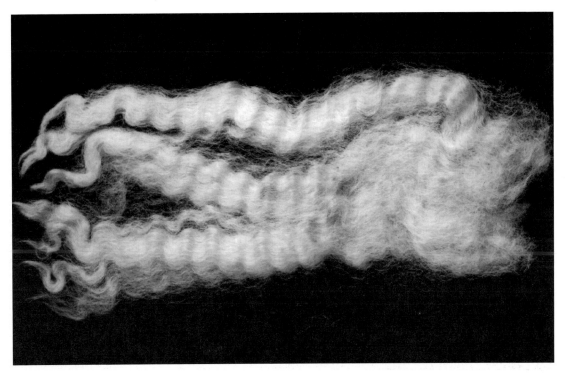

The Borderdale is the result of cross-breeding Border Leicester with Corriedale. It is a dual-purpose breed, intended to produce good wool weights and prime lamb hindquarters.

The sheep are medium to large with clean white faces and legs, and wool on the poll. The breed is particularly well suited to rolling hill country and irrigated pastures.

The fine crossbred wool has firm oval to rectangular staples with pointed tips. Borderdale fleece is commercially used in handknitting yarns and heavyweight apparel, and it is popular with handspinners.

Fleece weight: 10–13 pounds (4.5 kg–6 kg)
Fiber diameter: 48s–54s (35μ–30μ)
Staple length: 4–6 inches (100 mm–150 mm)
Found in: New Zealand

This breed originated in New Zealand. A hairy Border Leicester × Romney ram was mated to coarse-fleeced Perendale ewes with the objective of producing fleece suited to the carpet industry. Because of its heavy, lean carcass, the Carpetmaster may be considered a dual-purpose breed.

The fiber is heavily medullated with little distinguishable crimp. Like other carpet-wool breeds, Carpetmasters are shorn twice yearly, when the fleece is a usable length.

Fleece weight: 6½–9 pounds (3 kg–4 kg) (six months' growth)
Fiber diameter: 36s–44s (41μ–38μ)
Staple length: 6 inches (150 mm) (six months' growth)
Found in: New Zealand, South Australia

COOPWORTH

The Coopworth was developed in New Zealand from Border Leicester and Romney stock. The breed, registered in 1968, takes its name from Ian Coop, a professor at Lincoln College, Canterbury, who initiated and headed the research from which it resulted. The aim was to produce sheep with high fertility and good lamb growth. High lambing percentages, easy care, and good mothering abilities combined with heavy fleece weight have made this an attractive dual-purpose breed. Strict breeding criteria are enforced to maintain a high standard of stock. The Coopworth flourishes on wetter lowlands and gentle hill country.

Coopworths are medium to large with white faces and legs; they usually have some wool on the poll. They look much like Perendales but lack the upright ears of that breed.

The fleece is lustrous, long, and spins freely. Staples may be round or flat.

Coopworth in its finer ranges can be used to make outer garments and upholstery whereas the stronger fiber is better suited to the production of rugs or carpets. Commercially, the wool is used in heavier apparel and carpets.

Fleece weight: 10–13 pounds (4.5 kg–6 kg)
Fiber diameter: 44s–48s (39μ–35μ)
Staple length: 5–7 inches (125 mm–175 mm)
Found in: New Zealand, Australia, Eastern Europe, United States

The Cotswold is an ancient breed which originated in the Cotswold Hills of Gloucestershire, England. Over the years Cotswold growth rate, conformation, and lamb weights have been improved with the addition of Lincoln and Leicester blood. The Cotswold is classified as a rare breed, but thanks to preservation efforts, its numbers are now increasing.

Like most luster longwools, Cotswolds are large, heavily built white-faced sheep similar to the Lincoln and English Leicester. Their faces are free from wool except for a tuft on the forehead. The heavy fleece is coarse and hangs in lustrous, wavy ringlets.

The natural luster of Cotswold gives dyed colors great life and depth. Hand-spinners will find the long-stapled fleece most suitable for use in heavy outerwear or hard-wearing rug and carpet yarns.

Fleece weight: 9–15 pounds (4 kg–7 kg)
Fiber diameter: 36s–46s (40μ–34μ)
Staple length: 7–12 inches (175 mm–300 mm)
Found in: United Kingdom, Canada, United States

Also known as the Gray-Faced Dartmoor, the Dartmoor is among the hardiest of the long-wool breeds, able to withstand the harsh conditions of the moorland pastures of southwest England.

These sheep have white faces with gray mottling. Their heads and legs are wooled, and both sexes are polled.

Dartmoor wool is curly and lustrous, and is one of the strongest of the longwools. It is most suitable for making hard-wearing carpet and rug yarns. Dartmoors are often shorn as lambs for their valuable first coat of warm, curly lamb's wool.

The Dartmoor has a close relative, the White Face Dartmoor, which may be distinguished by its white woolless face. The rams may be horned. It, too, thrives on exposed moorlands and has the same type and quality of fleece as the original Dartmoor.

Fleece weight: 13–17½ pounds (6 kg–8 kg)
Fiber diameter: 36s–40s (40+μ–36μ)
Staple length: 6–8 inches (150 mm–200 mm)
Found in: United Kingdom

DEVON AND CORNWALL LONGWOOL

This is a recent amalgamation of two old and very similar breeds, both of which originated in southwestern England. Although not the largest of the long-wool sheep, this breed produces some of the heaviest fleeces of the British breeds.

These sheep have white faces with black nostrils, and their heads and legs are well covered with wool. Both sexes are polled.

The lustrous fleece is very coarse and falls into large, open, curly locks. Like the Dartmoor, Devon and Cornwall lambs are often shorn at six months for their warm, resilient lamb's wool, which is used for knitwear and woven garment fabrics. Adult fleeces are most suitable for rug and carpet yarns.

Fleece weight: 15–22 pounds (7 kg–10 kg)
Fiber diameter: 32s–40s (40+μ–36μ)
Staple length: 8–12 inches (200 mm–300 mm)
Found in: United Kingdom, Australia, South Africa, South America

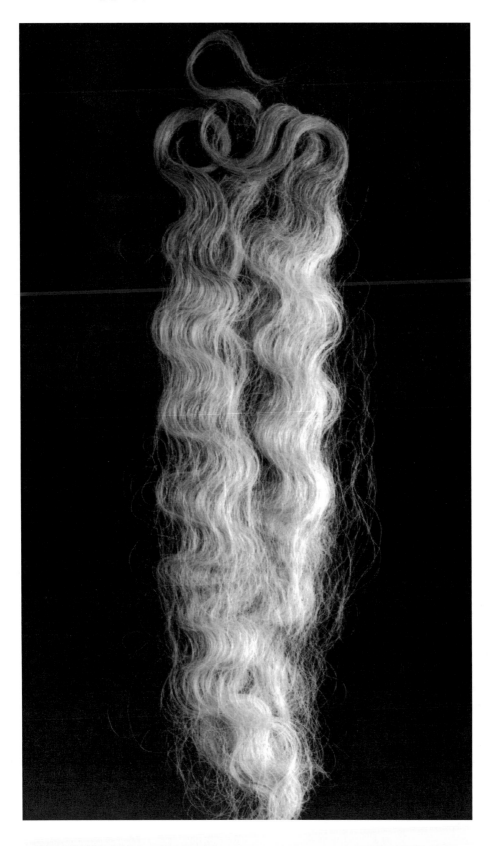

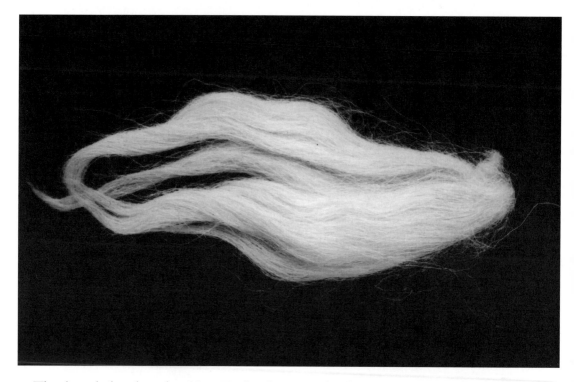

This breed, developed in New Zealand, began as a strain of Romney selected for its hairiness, a factor usually undesirable to wool growers. Under the guidance of Francis Dry of Massey Agricultural College, Palmerston North, very hairy Romneys were studied for twenty-five years. A single gene that stimulates the production of the medullated fibers sought by carpet manufacturers was recognized to be the source of hairy birthcoats in Romney lambs. Drysdale has now mostly replaced the imported Scottish Blackface that was used as the basis for the New Zealand carpet industry.

Drysdales are medium-large and have white faces and legs. The rams are heavily horned whereas the ewes have short horns.

The fleece contains three types of fiber: kemp (very short and coarse, about 10 percent of the weight); long, coarse medullated fibers (about 65 percent), and fine, nonmedullated fibers (about 25 percent). A year's growth produces a very long triangular-shaped staple, but because it is difficult to process, Drysdales are shorn twice yearly.

Fleece weight: 11–15 pounds (5 kg–7 kg) (six months' growth)
Fiber diameter: 36s (40+μ)
Staple length: 8–12 inches (200 mm–300 mm) (six months' growth)
Found in: New Zealand, Australia

An Australian development of Drysdale, Border Leicester, and Merino blood resulted in the Elliottdale, a carpet-wool breed.

These sheep are medium-sized and white, with semi-open faces. The rams and most of the ewes are horned.

The fleece has a high proportion of medullated fiber, and the staple shows virtually no crimp. Sheep are shorn twice a year to ensure fiber of a manageable length for processing.

Fleece weight: 6½–9 pounds (3 kg–4 kg) (six months' growth)
Fiber diameter: 36s–44s (41μ–38μ)
Staple length: 5–7 inches (120 mm–180 mm) (six months' growth)
Found in: Australia

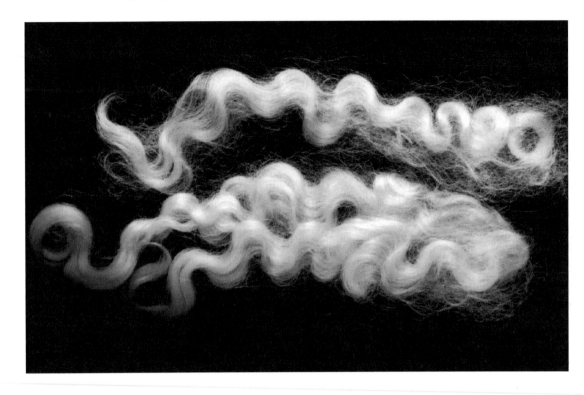

This long-established British breed has contributed much to improving many other longwools. During the eighteenth century, the breed was considerably improved by Robert Bakewell, a pioneer in the field of animal genetics. He selectively bred to produce a smaller, shorter sheep which fattened well at an earlier age.

English Leicesters are large and have clean faces, dark noses and lips, and forelocks on the poll. The fleece is long, heavy, lustrous, and of consistent length and fiber diameter. The staples are deeply waved and very flat with pointed tips. English Leicester wool is used commercially in the manufacture of braids, coatings, suit linings, upholstery, and rugs.

Fleece weight: 11–14 pounds (5 kg–6.5 kg)
Fiber diameter: 40s–46s (40μ–37μ)
Staple length: 6–8 inches (150 mm–250 mm)
Found in: United Kingdom, Australia, New Zealand, United States

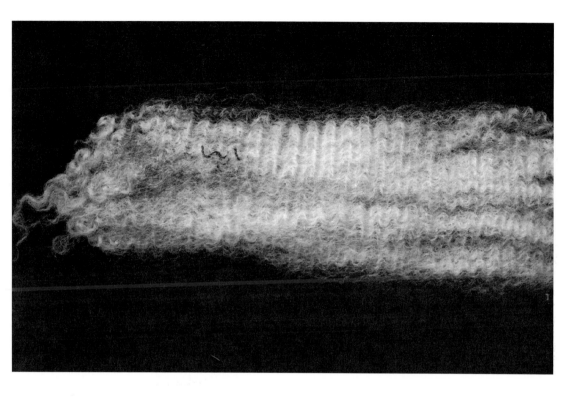

Also known as Finn or Finnsheep, the Finnish Landrace, a native of Finland and one of several breeds originating from the Scandinavian short-tailed sheep, is thought to have been in existence for several hundred years. This hardy breed thrives in rugged climates and on high-roughage feed. Finnish Landrace sheep are valued primarily for their ability to produce multiple lambs early and often, and are used to enhance lambing performance in crossbred ewes. The sheep have naturally short tails.

The fleece is semilustrous and very open, and the staples have long, pointed tips which may be brittle or tangled. In some areas, they are shorn twice a year to preserve fleece quality. The crimp is variable, but all fleeces should have a silky handle.

Finnish Landrace fleece is suitable for a wide range of knitted and woven fabrics including sweaters and other outer garments, blankets, and throws. The crimp adds bounce to blends with mohair, alpaca, or llama while the silky handle preserves softness and luster.

Fleece weight: 4–8 pounds (1.8 kg–3.6 kg)
Fiber diameter: 50s–60s (31μ–24μ)
Staple length: 3–6 inches (75 mm–150 mm)
Found in: Scandinavia, Canada, France, United States, New Zealand

Also known as Palsäu, Gotland sheep were developed from the original Swedish short-tailed sheep on the Island of Gotland in the Baltic Sea. The breed has been improved through selection for meat production and gray pelts, and is now a major breed in Sweden.

Gotland sheep are medium-sized, lean and leggy with dark heads and legs. The lambs are born black but become lighter with age except for their faces, legs, and a dark line along the back.

The fleece is lustrous and silky. The locks are small with a wavy or open curly crimp. Unlike most other crossbred wools, Gotland has a tendency to felt, so take care to avoid aggitating the fleece when washing it. Gotland wool is suitable for use in knitted and woven outerwear. Its principal commercial use is as lamb pelts for the fur garment industry.

Fleece weight: About 11 pounds (5 kg)
Fiber diameter: 48s–52s (32μ–28μ)
Staple length: 3–5 inches (80 mm–130 mm)
Found in: Sweden, Norway, New Zealand

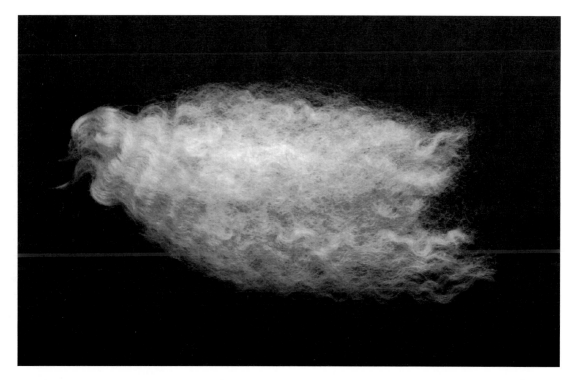

The Gromark was developed in New South Wales, Australia, in 1965. Border Leicester rams were crossed with Corriedale ewes and the offspring interbred. The aim was to produce an easy-care breed which would do well in a country with medium to high rainfall. The emphasis was placed on producing lean, heavy lambs while maintaining a good heavy fleece.

Gromarks are large, with white faces and clean legs. The wool is a fine crossbred type, and the staples are oval with pointed tips. The wool is similar to that of the Border-dale, which evolved from similar parentage.

Fleece weight: 9–11 pounds (4 kg–5 kg)
Fiber diameter: 46s–54s (34μ–28μ)
Staple length: 5–6 inches (120 mm–145 mm)
Found in: Australia

The Lincoln breed, named for the County of Lincolnshire, England, has been established since 1750 and is considered to be the foundation of all the British longwools. Lincolns have been used in the development of many other breeds in Australia (Polwarth and Zenith), New Zealand (Corriedale), and the United States (Targhee and Columbia).

Lincolns have large, broad, white faces and woolly white legs. Long forelocks from the poll hang over their faces.

The wool is very long, strong, and lustrous. Staples are firm, flat or oval, and have pointed tips.

Commercial uses are upholstery and wig making. Its luster and relatively soft handle for a strong wool make it very desirable for blending with mohair to create a yarn with less than 100 percent mohair but with the same or similar characteristics.

Fleece weight: 11–15 pounds (5 kg–7 kg)
Fiber diameter: 36s–40s (38μ–36μ)
Staple length: 7–10 inches (175 mm–250 mm)
Found in: England, Argentina, Australia, New Zealand, United States, other countries throughout the world

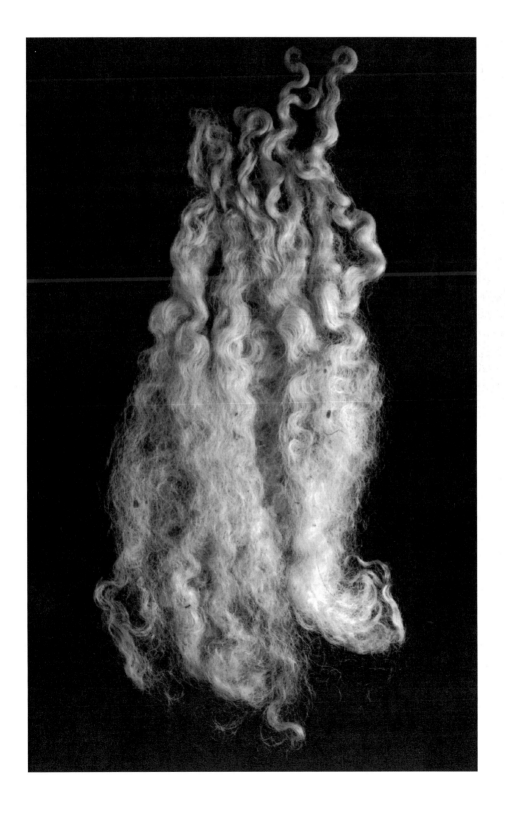

The Masham is the result of crossing a Teeswater or Wensleydale ram with a Dalesbred or Swaledale ewe. Ewes are hardy and prolific, producing good crossbred lambs; Mashams produce a heavy longwool fleece.

The sheep have distinctive black-and-white faces and legs, and small, woolly top-knots.

Masham fleece is lustrous, without kemps, and largely free from colored fibers, but the length and diameter of the wool can vary widely. Finer Masham fleeces are suitable for making outer garments. Stronger fleeces do well for upholstery, rugs, and carpets.

Fleece weight: 6½–9 pounds (3 kg–4 kg)
Fiber diameter: 46s–50s (34μ–29μ)
Staple length: 6–14 inches (150 mm–360 mm)
Found in: United Kingdom

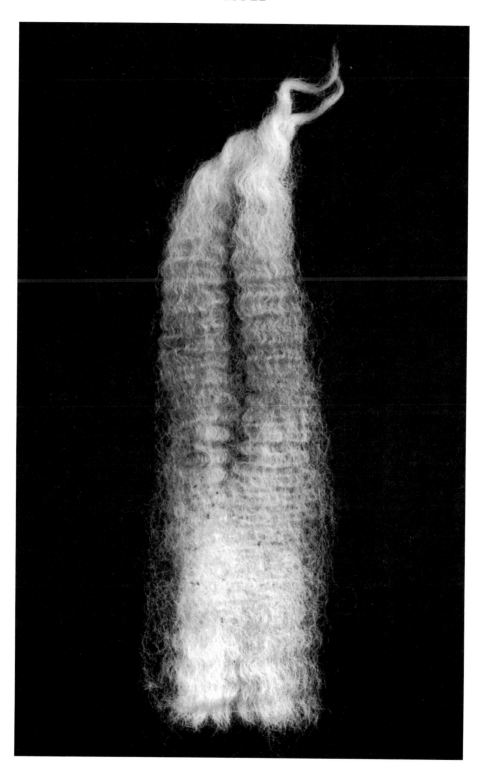

The North of England Mule (North English Mule) is the result of crossing a Blue-Faced Leicester ram with a Swaledale or Scottish Blackface ewe. This has become a very popular crossbred in the United Kingdom and accounts for more than 20 percent of the British wool clip.

Mules are polled with mottled faces and legs that are free of wool.

The fleece is semilustrous with a fine, wavy crimp that gives good loft. The staples are long and have pointed tips.

The comparatively light, airy feel of this longwool fleece makes it a good choice for the production of hard-wearing but warm knitted and woven outerwear. Stronger fleeces are suitable for use in upholstery and rug yarns.

The Welsh Mule is a cross of a Blue-Faced Leicester ram with a ewe of one of the Welsh hill breeds such as the Welsh Mountain, Welsh Hill Speckled-Face, or Beulah Speckled-Face. The Welsh Mule is similar to the "classic" Mule except that the wool may be a little finer and shorter: 50s–56s (31μ–26μ) and 4–8 inches (100 mm–200 mm).

Fleece weight: 5½–8 pounds (2.5 kg–3.6 kg)
Fiber diameter: 46s–54s (34μ–28μ)
Staple length: 4–10 inches (100 mm–250 mm)
Found in: United Kingdom

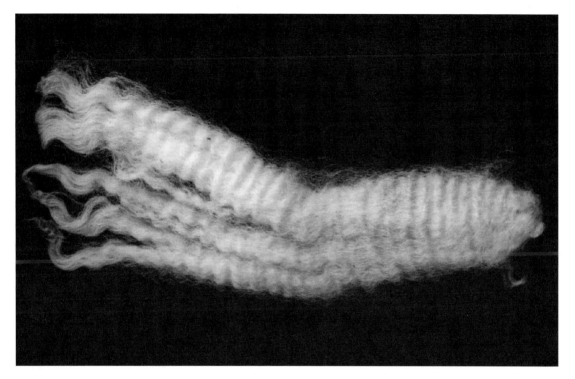

This dual-purpose breed was developed in New Zealand by Sir Geoffrey Peren of Massey Agricultural College, Palmerston North, from whom it takes its name. Cheviot and Romney stock were interbred to produce this easy-care sheep. The breed was first registered in 1960 and has since become a popular choice for hill country farming as the sheep thrive on poor pasture and are easy to herd.

Perendales are small to medium sheep. They have clean white faces and legs with some wool on the poll. Their noses are black and their ears upright. They resemble Coopworth but can be distinguished by their ears.

Perendale fleece is noted for its bulk and low luster. The staples have rather open, pointed tips and are usually oval. Its springiness makes the finer Perendale fiber ideal for use in knitwear and blankets, whereas the stronger fiber is used in carpet making.

Fleece weight: 7½–11 pounds (3.5 kg–5 kg)
Fiber diameter: 48s–56s (35μ–28μ)
Staple length: 4–6 inches (100 mm–150 mm)
Found in: New Zealand, Southeastern Australia

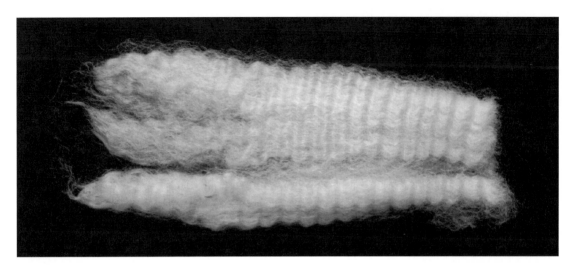

Romneys evolved on the Romney Marshes in Kent, England. A large, flat area of reclaimed seabed, the area is swept by wind and rain. Over the centuries, the sheep have developed resistance to foot rot and parasites, conditions common in sheep that are kept on wet ground. Romneys have been exported to many countries, but nowhere have they become as important as in New Zealand, where in the 1960s three-quarters of the national flock of 50,000,000 were Romneys. Through breeding improvements, New Zealand Romneys are heavier fleeced animals than the original stock imported from Britain.

The Romney has been used to develop new breeds (such as the Perendale, Coopworth, and Romeldale), and hairy mutant types have been used to develop carpet-wool breeds (such as the Drysdale and Tukidale).

Romneys are medium-sized sheep with white faces and woolly legs. They have black noses and their faces are clear about the eyes.

The fiber has some luster and a well-defined crimp. The staples are oval or round and have pointed tips, which are more pronounced on the stronger wool. The strong or coarse fleece (about 60 percent of the clip) is used by the carpet industry whereas the finer fleece goes into blankets, upholstery, and knitted outer garments.

Romney (Romney Marsh or Kent)
Fleece weight: 6½–10 pounds (3 kg–4.5 kg)
Fiber diameter: 48s–54s (35μ–30μ)
Staple length: 4–8 inches (100 mm–200 mm)
Found in: Most sheep-growing countries of the world.

New Zealand Romney
Fleece weight: 10–13 pounds (4.5 kg–6 kg)
Fiber diameter: 46s–50s (37μ–33μ)
Staple length: 5–7 inches (125 mm–175 mm)
Found in: Most sheep-growing countries of the world.

TEESWATER

The Teeswater is a luster long-wool breed that resembles the Wensleydale in appearance and fleece type. The Teeswater is generally thought to be more suitable for meat production than the Wensleydale, and it is used extensively to cross with other breeds (such as the Swaledale, Dalesbred, and Rough Fell) to produce the Masham crossbred.

Teeswaters have light gray faces with darker mottling on their noses and legs. They have curly forelocks. Both sexes are polled.

Teeswater wool is one of the finer long-wools and has very good luster. The staples are long with tapered tips, and they form a mass of small curly locks.

This is a good long-wool fleece for use in garments or to produce special-effect yarns in which luster and strength are important.

Fleece weight: 7½–15 pounds (3.5 kg–7 kg)
Fiber diameter: 44s–50s (36μ–30μ)
Staple length: 6–12 inches (150 mm–300 mm)
Found in: United Kingdom

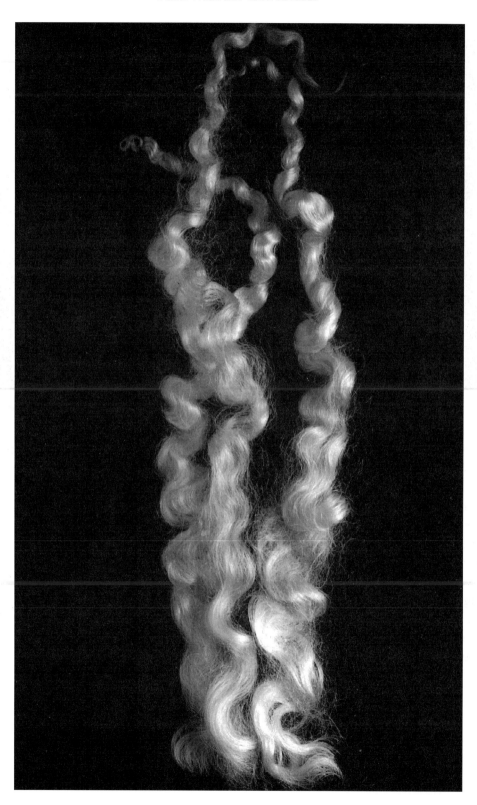

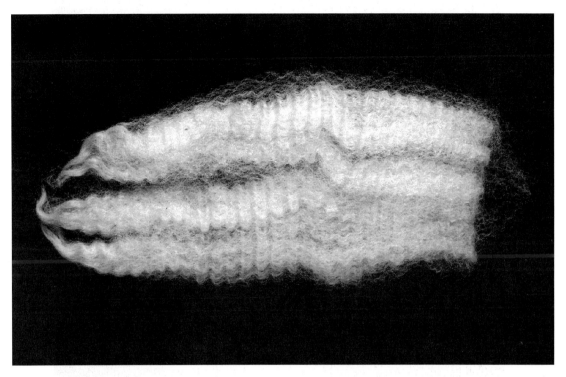

The modern Texel was developed in the Netherlands in the late nineteenth and early twentieth centuries by crossing the local (Old Texel) sheep with British longwools. It is the most numerous breed in the Netherlands, where it is valued as a sire for crossbred market lambs and for its fleece.

Texels have clean, white faces and legs, and both sexes are polled.

Texel wool is medium to coarse with average loft and very little luster. Many fleeces have a high proportion of kemp; this is something to watch out for when selecting a fleece. The moderate, even staple length makes it suitable for all preparation methods.

Finer fleeces are well suited to the making of knitted and woven outer garments and blankets. Coarser fleeces will make hard-wearing rugs and carpets.

Fleece weight: 8–12 pounds (3.6 kg–5.5 kg)
Fiber diameter: 46s–56s (34μ–26μ)
Staple length: 3–6 inches (80 mm–150 mm)
Found in: Netherlands, Canada, France, Germany, United Kingdom, United States, New Zealand

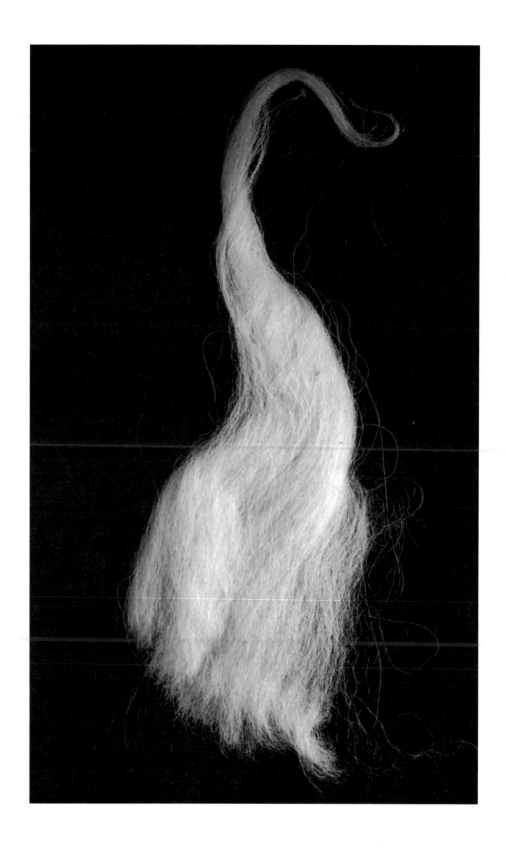

The Tukidale was developed in New Zealand after the out-of-season birth of a mutant, hairy ram from a Romney ewe. Drysdales were being bred to provide wool for the carpet industry but initially the rams were hired to the carpet companies who in turn leased them to farmers, under contract to sell the wool they produced back to these companies. It was some time before private breeders were able to obtain Drysdale rams so it was decided to breed from the ram born on "TukiTuki", and it is from the farm where it originated that the breed took its name.

Tukidales have white, semi-open faces and lightly wooled faces, ears, and legs; both sexes are horned.

The fleece is similar to that of the Drysdale and the staples are oval with very pointed, hairy tips. Shearing is twice yearly and Tukidale fleece is used in the commercial manufacture of carpets. Handspinners too would find it suitable as yarn for rug weaving or any other floor covering.

Fleece weight: 6½–9 pounds (3 kg–4 kg) (6 month's growth)
Fiber diameter: 36s and coarser (35μ–45μ)
Staple length: 6 inches (150 mm)
Found in: New Zealand, Australia

Wensleydales are large-bodied sheep with distinctive blue-gray faces. Like the very similar Teeswaters, they have curly forelocks, and both sexes are polled.

The principal use of Wensleydales is to provide rams for crossing with other breeds, particularly with the Swaledale, Rough Fell, and Scottish Blackface. A Wensleydale ram crossed with a Swaledale or Dalesbred ewe produces the Masham.

The fleece is one of the finest of the luster longwools and falls from the body in a mass of small, loosely curling ringlets. The staples are long, tapered, silky, and very lustrous.

Commercially, Wensleydale wool is used to produce fabrics with a lustrous finish or linings, and it is sometimes blended with shorter wools to add strength. Because it is finer and softer than many of the other luster longwools, it is a good choice for garment fabrics and special-effect yarns in which luster and long staple length can be used to advantage.

Fleece weight: 9–15 pounds (4 kg–7 kg)
Fiber diameter: 44s–50s (36μ–30μ)
Staple length: 8–12 inches (200 mm–300 mm)
Found in: United Kingdom

4
DOWN-TYPE WOOLS

Clun Forest ewe lamb.
Photograph by Bets Reedy.

In this category, we have included not only the true down breeds that originated in southeastern England (Southdown, Suffolk Down, Hampshire Down, Dorset Down, Oxford Down, and Shropshire Down), but also the other short-wooled sheep that share the same fleece characteristics, if not the same ancestral locality. Many of the British hill breeds have similar fleeces, and are included in this group where appropriate.

Down-type sheep are bred principally for use as sires of crossbred fat lambs. For this reason, breeders usually place primary em-phasis on superior meat quality, confor-mation, and growth rate. Sheep are gener-ally compact and medium-sized, with ei-ther white or dark faces and legs.

The wool has a distinctive crisp feel and a full, spongy handle. It ranges in fiber di-ameter from fine to medium and is gener-ally between 2 and 3½ inches (50 mm and 80 mm) long. The fibers are long compared to the length of the staple because of a well-developed spiral crimp. Although in-distinct in the staples, the crimp con-tributes to the wool's excellent resilience, loft, bulk, and elasticity. The blocky or rectangular staples themselves are usually poorly defined. The fleece, typically without luster, is described as chalky. Many of the down-type breeds may produce colored and kemp fibers in their fleeces; this is something to watch out for when selecting a fleece for handspinning.

Commercially, down-type wools are used principally to make tweeds, blankets, and hosiery. The remarkable springiness and resilience of the fiber results in good shape retention and insulation, as well as excellent crease resistance. As handspinners, we can make use of the same qualities in sweaters, socks, throws, blankets, and gar-ment fabrics by using down-type fleece alone or blended with other wools.

Down-type breeds vary in the handle of their fleeces. Southdown, South Dorset Down, and Dorset tend to produce relatively fine, soft fleeces, suitable for socks and finer fabrics. Most of the breeds fall in the middle range and are good for making knitted outerwear, long-wearing woven garments, and blankets. The coarsest of the down-type fleeces can be blended with long-wool or crossbred wools to add resilience and body to upholstery fabrics and carpet yarns.

Montadale lock and yarn samples. Clockwise from upper left: two-ply spun from flick-carded locks; three-ply spun with a short draw from drum-carded batts; two-ply spun with a short draw from drum-carded batts.

Singles yarn woolen-spun from hand-carded Clun Forest fleece and woven in a goose-eye twill.

WASHING

Down-type wool does not felt easily and requires no more than reasonable care in washing. The grease content is generally moderate and will remain fluid unless the fleece is stored for a long period. It will wash out easily with hot water and detergent. Because they are open and airy, down fleeces dry quickly. Don't be alarmed if the staple seems shorter after washing—the fiber hasn't shrunk. Washing causes the crimp to curl up even more, leaving you with a slightly shorter staple. You may wish to select your preparation method after washing so that you can see what length of staple you will be working with.

PREPARATION

Although down fleeces are in theory suitable for any preparation method, staple length dictates that some approaches will be more successful than others. For the very short fleeces, hand- and drum-carding are most efficient. Those fleeces that are long enough, usually about 3 inches (76 mm), can also be flick-carded or combed with good results. Short fibers will need more spinning twist to anchor them firmly in the yarn. Because these fleeces tend to be very bouncy, you may not notice a great difference in appearance between a yarn spun from carded wool and one spun from combed fiber. The real difference will come in the greater durability of the combed fiber.

This crocheted swatch capitalizes on the loft of down-type fleeces to create a blanket fabric that is both warm and lightweight.

The resilient, spongy nature of down wools and the softness of this fine Dorset fleece are an ideal combination for comfortable socks.

QUICK REFERENCE GUIDE TO DOWN–TYPE WOOL

Breed	Softness	Elasticity & Loft	Staple Length	Luster	Felting Properties
Beulah Speckled Face	◆◆	◆◆◆◆	◆◆◆	◆▾	
Black Welsh Mtn	◆	◆◆◆▾	◆◆	◆◆	◆▾
British Milk Sheep	◆◆	◆◆◆◆	◆◆◆▾		
Cheviot	◆◆	◆◆◆▾	◆◆◆	◆▾	◆
Clun Forest	◆◆◆	◆◆◆◆◆	◆◆	◆	◆
Colbred	◆▾	◆◆◆▾	◆◆◆▾	◆▾	
Derbyshire Gritstone	◆◆	◆◆◆◆	◆◆▾	◆▾	◆
Devon Closewool	◆▾	◆◆◆▾	◆◆◆	◆▾	
Dorset Down	◆◆◆	◆◆◆◆◆	◆	◆	◆
Dorset Horn & Poll	◆◆	◆◆◆◆▾	◆◆▾	◆▾	◆
Exmoor Horn	◆◆	◆◆◆▾	◆◆◆	◆▾	
Hampshire Down	◆◆▾	◆◆◆◆◆	◆	◆	◆
Hill Radnor	◆◆	◆◆◆▾	◆◆◆▾	◆▾	
Kerry Hill	◆◆▾	◆◆◆◆	◆◆▾	◆▾	
Llanwenog	◆◆	◆◆◆◆	◆◆	◆	
Lleyn	◆◆▾	◆◆◆◆	◆◆◆	◆▾	
Lonk	◆▾	◆◆◆◆	◆◆◆▾	◆▾	
Montadale	◆◆◆	◆◆◆▾	◆◆◆	◆◆▾	◆◆
Norfolk Horn	◆◆▾	◆◆◆◆▾	◆◆▾		
Oxford Down	◆◆	◆◆◆◆◆	◆◆◆	◆▾	◆▾
Portland	◆◆	◆◆◆▾	◆▾		
Ryeland	◆◆◆	◆◆◆◆	◆◆▾	◆▾	◆▾
Shetland	◆◆◆	◆◆◆▾	◆◆▾	◆◆	◆◆▾
Shropshire	◆◆▾	◆◆◆◆◆	◆◆▾	◆	◆
South Dorset Down	◆◆◆	◆◆◆◆◆	◆	◆	◆
Southdown	◆◆◆	◆◆◆◆◆	◆	◆	◆
South Hampshire	◆◆◆	◆◆◆◆◆	◆	◆	◆
South Suffolk	◆◆◆	◆◆◆◆◆	◆	◆	◆
South Wales Mountain	◆	◆◆◆▾	◆	◆▾	
Suffolk	◆◆▾	◆◆◆◆◆	◆	◆	◆
Tunis	◆◆◆	◆◆◆▾	◆◆◆	◆▾	◆◆
Welsh Hill Speckled	◆◆	◆◆◆▾	◆◆◆		
Welsh Mountain	◆	◆◆◆	◆◆▾	◆▾	
Welsh Mtn Badger	◆▾	◆◆◆▾	◆◆▾	◆▾	◆▾
Whitefaced Woodland	◆◆	◆◆◆▾	◆◆◆▾		

Five diamonds indicate the maximum amount of the quality.

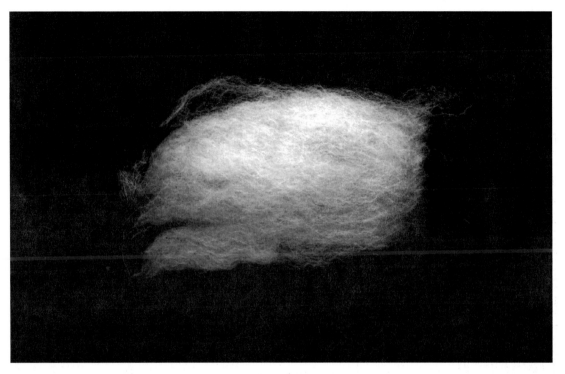

This Welsh hill breed has the rather imposing full name of Epynt Hill And Beulah Speckled-Face. It has developed in the hill country of central and western Wales and is well known as a good mother and excellent milker.

As the name suggests, these sheep have distinct black-and-white speckled faces; their legs are free from wool. They are a little larger than the true Welsh mountain breeds, and both sexes are polled.

The resilient, springy wool is finer than that of the mountain breeds. Finer fleeces are suitable for making pliant, crush-resistant garments whereas the strong fleeces are more appropriate for use in upholstery fabrics and carpet yarns.

Fleece weight: 3¹/₂–4¹/₂ pounds (1.5 kg–2 kg)
Fiber diameter: 50s–56s (31µ–26µ)
Staple length: 3–5 inches (80 mm–120 mm)
Found in: United Kingdom

This breed is remarkable for its all-black fleece. These are small sheep, with black faces and legs that are free from wool. The ewes are polled, and the rams are horned.

The fleece is coarse to medium with moderate luster and good loft. The fleece is used only in the specialty wool industry, in which it can be used by itself and blended with other fleeces to produce patterned fabrics in natural colors.

It is suitable for the production of outerwear, upholstery fabrics, and rugs.

Fleece weight: 3–4 pounds (1.2 kg–1.8 kg)
Fiber diameter: 48s–56s (33µ–26µ)
Staple length: 3–4 inches (80 mm–100 mm)
Found in: United Kingdom, Europe

This is a relatively recent breed, developed for good lambing performance and high milk production. British Milk Sheep have white faces and legs, which are free from wool.

The staples are oblong in shape with short tapered tips. The heavy, medium fleece is used commercially to make hand-knitting yarns and hosiery. Handspinners will find it useful for lofty, knitted and woven fabrics.

Fleece weight: 9–11 pounds (4 kg–5 kg)
Fiber diameter: 50s–54s (31μ–28μ)
Staple length: $4^1/_2$–7 inches (120 mm–180 mm)
Found in: United Kingdom, Europe

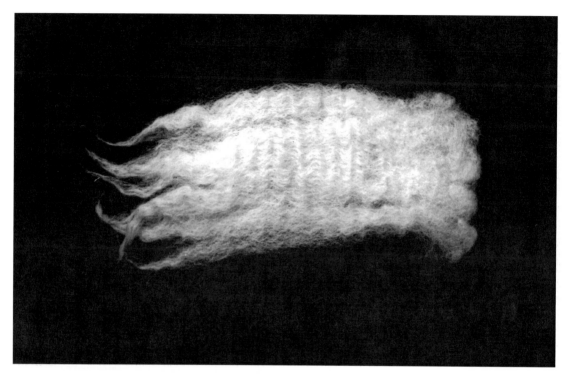

Ancestors of this breed have roamed the hills of Scotland and the border country between Scotland and England for centuries. The North Country Cheviot is a larger and less hardy animal than the Border or South Country Cheviot, which is noted for its compact formation and erect ears.

Cheviot faces are clean and white; their legs are short and free of wool.

The resilient, bulky fleece produces lofty yarn. Its staples are rectangular, with slightly pointed tips. The wool is resilient and airy, but not as quite as spongy as a true down fleece. Because some Cheviot wool is harsh, it is often overlooked by handspinners.

Commercial uses include the manufacture of tweeds, blankets, knitwear, and hosiery yarns. Stronger fleece is used by the carpet industry.

Fleece weight: 4½–6½ pounds (2 kg–3 kg)
Fiber diameter: 48s–56s (33μ–28μ)
Staple length: 3–5 inches (75 mm–125 mm)
Found in: United Kingdom, Australia, Canada, New Zealand, South Africa, United States, Scandinavia

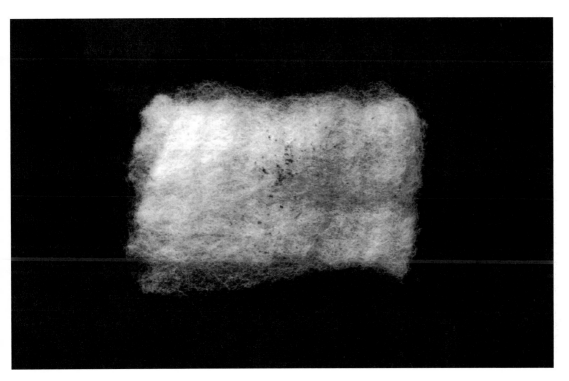

These sheep originated in the Welsh border area of Britain, probably from a mixture of the Shropshire and Ryeland breeds. They have high fertility and make good mothers.

The Clun Forest has a dark brown face and legs and a woolly forelock. Both sexes are polled.

Clun Forest wool has the usual characteristics of down fleeces (short staple, low luster, and a fine, elastic crimp), but it is also dense, fine, uniform throughout the fleece, and relatively free from colored fibers and kemp. The high quality of the fleece makes the Clun Forest more of a dual-purpose, down-type breed.

In industry, the wool is used for a wide range of goods, including hosiery, flannels, knitting yarns, fine tweeds, and industrial felts. Handspinners can put the fine, bouncy wool to good use in socks, mittens, crush-resistant woven fabrics, or blend it with other medium-to-fine wools and fibers for added loft and elasticity.

Fleece weight: $4^{1}/_{2}$–$6^{1}/_{2}$ pounds (2 kg–3 kg)
Fiber diameter: 56s–58s (28μ–25μ)
Staple length: $2^{1}/_{2}$–4 inches (60 mm–100 mm)
Found in: United Kingdom, Canada, United States

Developed in the Cotswold hills in the 1950s, the Colbred is raised principally for lambing performance and good milk production.

Colbreds are medium to large, white-faced sheep with legs and faces clear of wool. Both sexes are polled. They produce a medium to coarse fleece that is down-like in character. It is suitable for warm, lofty outer wear.

Fleece weight: $5\frac{1}{2}$–$7\frac{1}{2}$ pounds (2.5 kg–3.5 kg)

Fiber diameter: 48s–56s (32μ–26μ)

Staple length: 4–7 inches (100 mm–180 mm)

Found in: United Kingdom

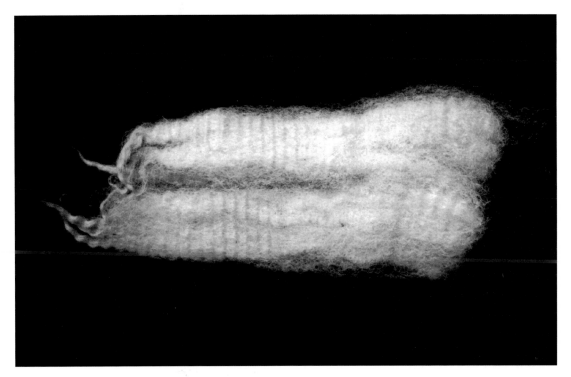

This breed originated in the Peak District of the Pennine Hills in Britain and is still found mostly in that area. It is one of the larger hill and mountain breeds and grows some of the finest wool of all the British blackface-type hill sheep.

Derbyshire Gritstones have black-and-white spotted wool-free faces and legs. Both sexes are polled.

The fleece is moderately open, with indistinct, blocky staples. The wool has a crisp handle and little luster. The crimp is pronounced and disorganized, giving the wool excellent loft and a light, airy feel.

When selecting a fleece, watch out for kemps and black fibers.

Gritstone wool has traditionally been used to make high-quality hosiery yarns. Handspinners will find it very versatile. It may be prepared using any method and produces light but warm blankets, knitwear, and woven fabrics.

Fleece weight: 5–6½ pounds (2.2 kg–3 kg)
Fiber diameter: 48s–56s (31μ–27μ)
Staple length: 4–6 inches (100 mm–150 mm)
Found in: United Kingdom

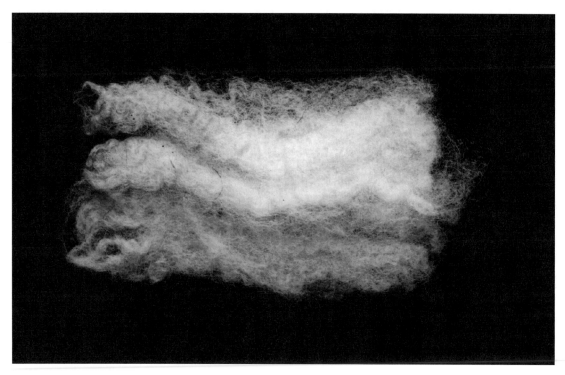

This hardy grassland sheep originated when the Devon Longwool was crossed with the Exmoor Horn. The Devon Closewool is a thrifty feeder and produces good lambs as well as a dense fleece of medium to strong down-type wool.

The sheep closely resemble the Exmoor Horn except that both sexes are polled. They are compact with white legs and faces, and wool on their heads and legs.

The fleece is a little coarser than that of the Exmoor Horn and has rectangular staples with short tips. It is tough and resilient and may be kempy, which makes it attractive for use in tweed fabrics. It would be a good choice for durable outerwear, upholstery fabrics, and carpets.

Fleece weight: 5–6½ pounds (2.2 kg–3 kg)
Fiber diameter: 46s–54s (34µ–28µ)
Staple length: 3–4½ inches (80 mm–120 mm)
Found in: United Kingdom

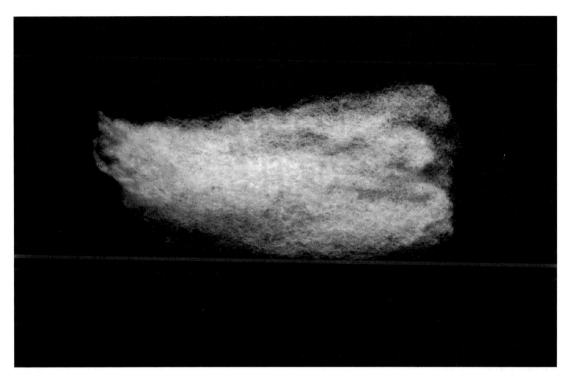

The Dorset Down takes its name from the English county where it was developed. Southdown rams were crossbred with ewes from a number of other breeds including Wiltshire and Hampshire with the aim of producing lean meat.

Dorset Downs are medium-sized with gray-brown faces, ears, and legs, and wool on the poll and cheeks.

The wool is fairly short, full-handling (but rather crisp) and springy, and is used in high-quality hosiery, knitwear, flannels, and fine tweed. It is often blended with other fleece types to add elasticity and crispness to yarn.

Fleece weight: 4½–6½ pounds (2 kg–3 kg)
Fiber diameter: 54s–58s (29μ–26μ)
Staple length: 2–3 inches (50 mm–75 mm)
Found in: England, Australia, Argentina, New Zealand, United States, and many other countries

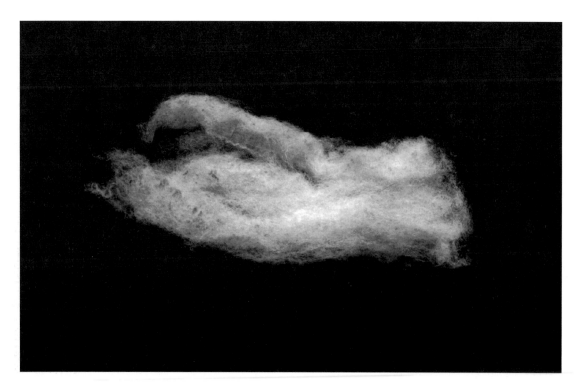

The Dorset Horn is a very old breed from the south of England; it bears very little resemblance to the Dorset Down. The Poll Dorset was developed in Australia by introducing the poll gene from Corriedale and Ryeland sheep. The Poll Dorset and Dorset are valued for their extended breeding season, early maturity, and good mothering.

Dorsets are medium-sized sheep, with pink skin and noses. Dorset Horn rams have heavy, curling horns; those of the ewes are lighter. Poll Dorsets resemble Dorset Horn sheep except, of course, for the absence of horns.

The wool is short, very white, spongy, and lacks luster, but it has a crisp handle. The staples are rectangular and have almost flat tips. As in the wool of the other down breeds, the crimp in the staple is very indistinct while the fiber itself is well but somewhat irregularly crimped.

This fiber is used commercially to make flannels, dress fabrics, and fine tweeds.

Fleece weight: $4\frac{1}{2}$–$6\frac{1}{2}$ pounds (2 kg–3 kg)
Fiber diameter: 50s–56s (32μ–27μ)
Staple length: 3–4 inches (75 mm–100 mm)
Found in: United Kingdom, Argentina, Australia, New Zealand, United States, South Africa, Canada

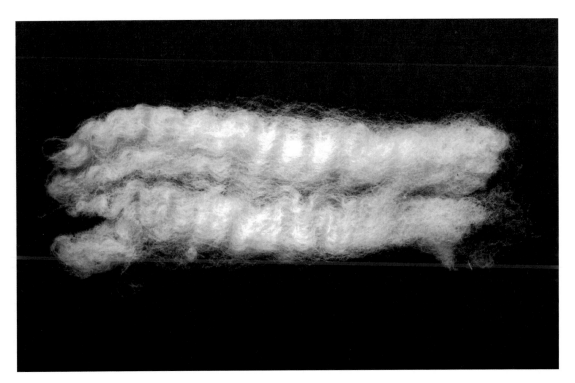

Exmoor Horns are compact, portly sheep, at home on the bleak pastures of their native Exmoor in southwestern England. They are hardy and thrifty, producing acceptable meat as well as good fleece of medium to strong wool.

The sheep have white faces with short forelocks and black nostrils. Their legs are white and are covered with wool. Both ewes and rams are horned.

Exmoor Horn fleece is similar to that of Cheviot and Welsh Mountain but a little stronger. It is dense and resilient with a full hand. It may have kemp but is free from colored fibers.

Commercially, the wool is used for hosiery, knitting yarns, tweeds, and felts. Handspinners will find it useful for making thick, lofty, fulled fabrics and rugged, warm outerwear.

Fleece weight: 5–7 pounds (2.2 kg–3.2 kg)
Fiber diameter: 48s–54s (32μ–28μ)
Staple length: 3–5 inches (80 mm–120 mm)
Found in: United Kingdom

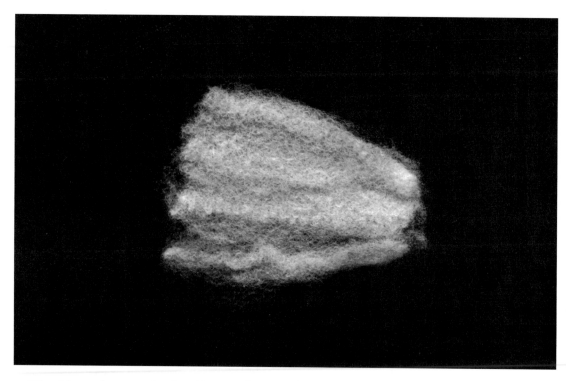

The Hampshire evolved in Britain from crosses of Southdown rams with large, slow maturing local ewes. It is primarily a lean meat breed.

Hampshires are large sheep. They have dark brown faces, ears, and legs with wool on the poll and cheeks. The staples are large and rectangular, with nearly flat tips. As with all other down-type fleece, the pronounced crimp is indistinct in the staple but very obvious in individual fibers. The fleece makes hardwearing, elastic, yarns for knitted or woven fabrics.

Fleece weight: 4$^{1}/_{2}$–6$^{1}/_{2}$ pounds (2 kg–3 kg)
Fiber diameter: 54s–58s (30μ–26μ)
Staple length: 2–3 inches (50 mm–75 mm)
Found in: England, Australia, New Zealand, South Africa, United States, Canada

This versatile sheep originated in the Welsh hills near the English border; it is probably an offshoot of the Welsh Mountain. It is more docile than most of the other Welsh mountain breeds, and it does as well in the hill country as it does in the lowlands.

Hill Radnor sheep are medium-sized animals with tan wool-free faces and legs. The rams have horns, but the ewes are polled.

The fleece is slightly crisp and dense. It tends to be kempy. The kemp and colored fibers make Hill Radnor an attractive choice if you want to spin tweedlike yarns for knitted and woven outerwear.

Fleece weight: $4\frac{1}{2}$–$5\frac{1}{2}$ pounds (2 kg–2.5 kg)
Fiber diameter: 48s–54s (33μ–28μ)
Staple length: 3–$5\frac{1}{2}$ inches (80 mm–140 mm)
Found in: United Kingdom

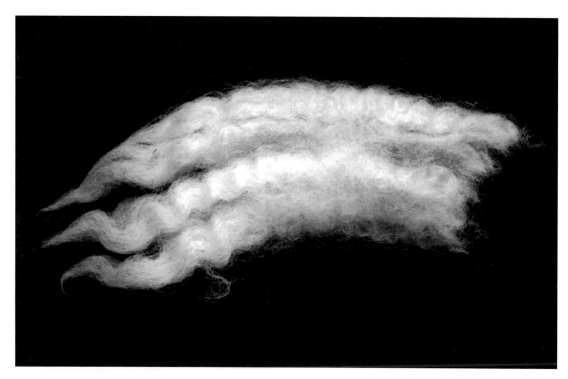

Named for the Kerry Hill area in Wales where the breed originated, Kerry Hill sheep are easily recognized by their distinctive white faces with sharply defined black patches on noses, eyes, ears, and legs. The heads and legs are free from wool, and both sexes are polled. The ewes are excellent mothers and are used to produce cross-bred lambs.

Kerry Hill fleece is dense, and it is one of the softest British fleeces. Some fleeces contain colored fibers and kemp. The softness and bounce of this wool makes it valuable for a wide variety of uses, including the production of knitting yarns, garment fabrics, and upholstery fabrics, as well as for blending with other wools and fibers.

Fleece weight: 5–6½ pounds (2.2 kg–3 kg)
Fiber diameter: 52s–56s (29μ–26μ)
Staple length: 2½–5 inches (60 mm–120 mm)
Found in: United Kingdom

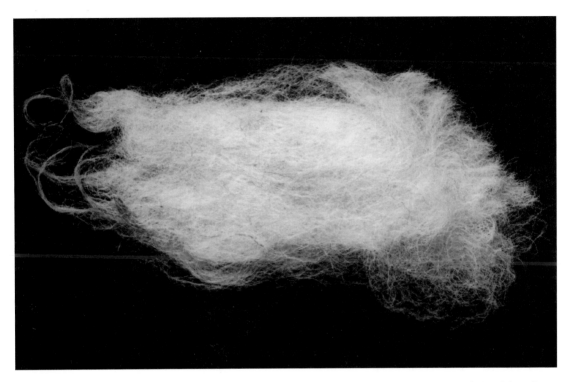

The Llanwenog originated in western Wales from a crossing of Shropshire rams with local black-faced ewes. Llanwenogs are prolific and do well on both the harsher upland country and lowland pastures.

The sheep have black heads and legs with a prominent tuft of wool on their foreheads. Both sexes are polled.

The wool is in the medium to fine range for down-type fleeces. It is suitable for sweaters and blankets, and for blending with other wools to produce sweaters, and woven garment fabrics.

Fleece weight: 4½–5½ pounds (2 kg–2.5 kg)
Fiber diameter: 56s–58s (28μ–25μ)
Staple length: 2–4 inches (60 mm–100 mm)
Found in: United Kingdom

This breed, developed on the Lleyn Peninsula of northwestern Wales, is well known for multiple births. The ewes breed early and are heavy milkers.

These hardy, medium-sized sheep have white faces and legs. They have no wool on their faces or lower legs, and both sexes are polled.

The wool has very little luster but contains no kemp and has good loft. It falls in the medium range and makes excellent bouncy yarns for knitwear and woven fabrics.

Fleece weight: $4\frac{1}{2}$–$6\frac{1}{2}$ pounds (2 kg–3 kg)
Fiber diameter: 50s–56s (31μ–26μ)
Staple length: 3–5 inches (80 mm–120 mm)
Found in: United Kingdom

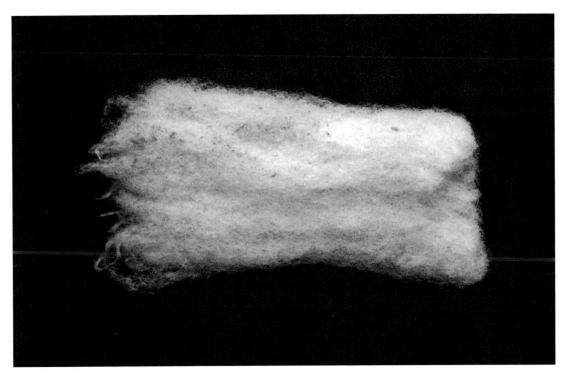

Lonk sheep evolved on the hillsides of the Pennine Chain of West Yorkshire. They are long-lived and produce better meat than most of the other mountain breeds.

Lonks have black-and-white mottled faces and legs that are clear of wool; both sexes are horned.

The fleece is medium to coarse with good bulk, and it is likely to contain some hair, kemp, and colored fibers. Finer grades are suitable for making knitted or woven outerwear fabrics and blankets, while stronger fleeces are excellent for carpet yarns.

Fleece weight: 5–6½ pounds (2.2 kg–3 kg)
Fiber diameter: 46s–54s (34μ–28μ)
Staple length: 4–6 inches (100 mm–150 mm)
Found in: United Kingdom

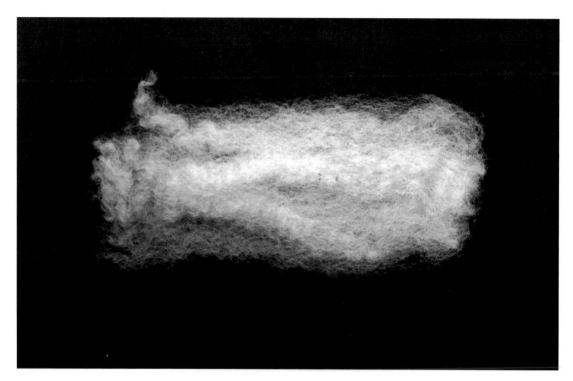

The Montadale is a dual-purpose breed developed in the United States in the 1930s from a foundation of Cheviot rams crossed with Columbia ewes. Breeding and selection for total weight of lamb and wool have resulted in a white-faced sheep that produces good meat and a fleece of medium wool with good spinning properties.

Montadales are hardy and they lamb easily. Both sexes are polled, and their faces and legs are free of wool.

The fleece is open and contains no pigmented fibers. The staples are blocky with slightly tapered tips. The crimp is well developed but indistinct, giving the wool a full, lofty handle with some crispness. It has almost no luster, but its loft makes Montadale wool an excellent choice for making warm but light outerwear and blankets.

Fleece weight: 8–12 pounds (3.6 kg–5.5 kg)
Fiber diameter: 54s–58s (30μ–25μ)
Staple length: 3–4½ inches (80 mm–110 mm)
Found in: United States, Canada

This now-rare breed was one of the original parents of the Suffolk. It has fallen from favor because its lambs mature slowly.

Norfolk Horns have dark faces and legs, both free from wool, and both sexes are horned. They grow a white, medium, down-type fleece with blocky staples and well-developed crimp. The wool is suitable for use in garment fabrics and blankets.

Fleece weight: 3½–4½ pounds (1.5 kg–2 kg)
Fiber diameter: 54s–56s (29μ–26μ)
Staple length: 3–4 inches (70 mm–100 mm)
Found in: United Kingdom

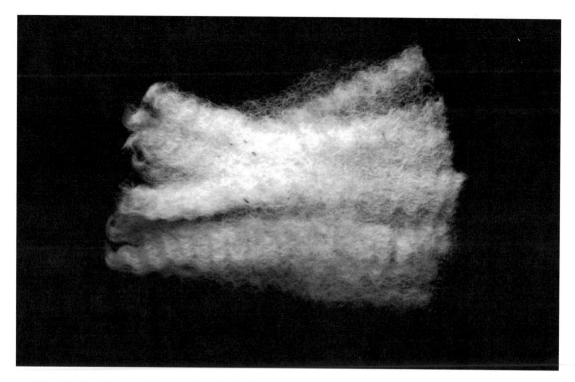

The Oxford Down (or simply Oxford, as it is known in some countries), is one of the largest of the down breeds. It originated in England about 1830 from crossings of Cotswold rams and Hampshire Down ewes, with some Southdown blood. They are prolific, and have good maternal instincts and mutton conformation. Their primary use is as sires for crossbreeding for meat production.

Oxfords have dark brown faces and legs with wool on their foreheads and cheeks. Oxfords have a typical medium down fleece with a staple that is slightly longer than usual. The wool is used commercially to make hosiery and handknitting yarns. Handspinners may find that the longer staple permits more flexibility in preparation and spinning methods than some of the other down-type wools.

Fleece weight: 6½–9 pounds (3 kg–4 kg)
Fiber diameter: 50s–54s (34μ–28μ)
Staple length: 3–5 inches (75 mm–125 mm)
Found in: United Kingdom, Canada, South America, United States, Continental Europe

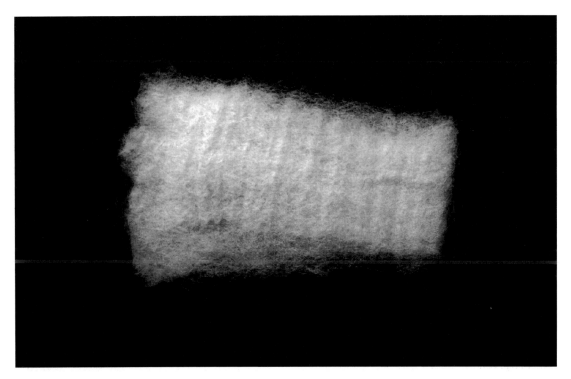

Now one of Britain's rare breeds, this small sheep was once highly prized for its superb meat. It has no wool on its tan face and lower legs, and both sexes are horned.

Portlands produce a medium to coarse fleece. The staples are blocky in shape and have square tips. The wool is suitable for the production of knitwear, woven outerwear, and blankets.

Fleece weight: $4^1/_2$–$6^1/_2$ pounds (2 kg–3 kg)
Fiber diameter: 50s–56s (31μ–26μ)
Staple length: $2^1/_2$–$3^1/_2$ inches (60 mm–90 mm)
Found in: United Kingdom

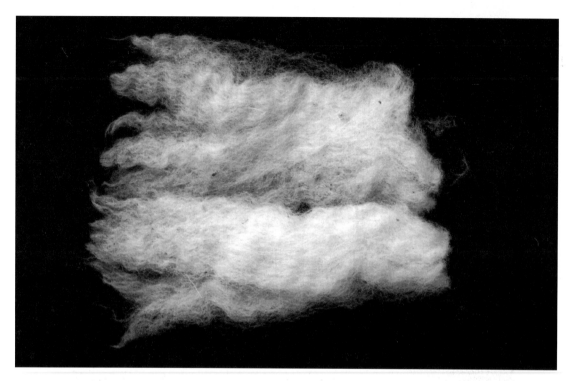

One of Britain's oldest breeds, the Ryeland has proved adaptable to many different types of pastures in other parts of the world. It is primarily a meat breed.

Ryelands are medium-sized and thickset. Their faces are white with wool on their foreheads and cheeks, and their legs are white and woolly.

The wool is a down type with a soft, light, springy handle; the fleeces contain very little kemp and few colored fibers. The staples are generally rectangular with tips that are almost flat. The crimp is rounded, although it may be rather indistinct.

Commercially, the wool is used alone or in blends with similar fleece for hosiery, handknitting wools, and high-quality smooth-finished tweeds.

Fleece weight: 6½–9 pounds (3 kg–4 kg)
Fiber diameter: 50s–56s (32μ–26μ)
Staple length: 3–4 inches (75 mm–100 mm)
Found in: United Kingdom, Australia, Canada, New Zealand, South America, elsewhere

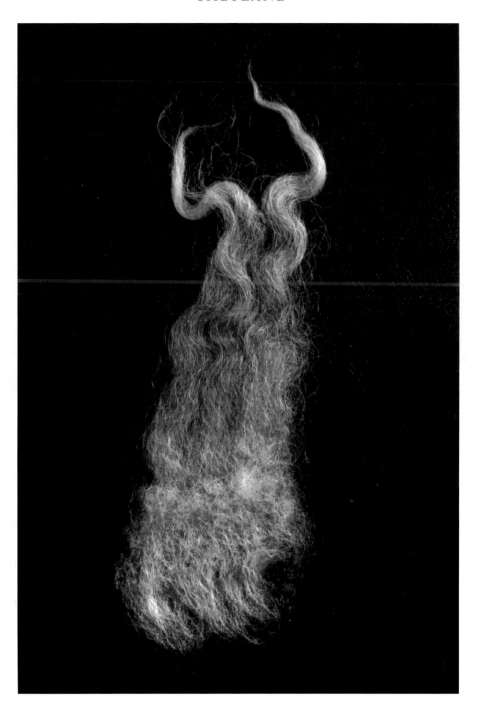

This small but very hardy breed evolved on the rugged, windswept Shetland Islands, almost halfway between Scotland and Norway. How and when the sheep arrived on the islands isn't known, but it seems likely that they were introduced by early Scandinavian settlers. The Shetland is a member of the northern short-tailed group of sheep and has the characteristic naturally short tail. Evidence of a slight double coat, a tendency to molt, and a rich variety of natural colors indicate close ties to primitive ancestors. In times past, the fleeces were plucked from the sheep (a procedure called *rooing*) during their natural molt, but now most fleeces are shorn.

Shetland has the finest wool among the British breeds, with a silky but slightly crisp hand. The staples are indistinct with tapered tips; the entire fleece is somewhat open. The wool doesn't have a noticeable luster, and the well-developed crimp gives it a light, airy feel.

Shetland wool has traditionally been used to make warm, rugged fabrics, including Fair Isle knitwear and woven tweeds. The famed handspun Shetland lace yarns are made from selected neck wool, which is considerably finer and softer than the rest of the fleece.

Fleece weight: 2¼–3½ pounds (1 kg–1.5 kg)
Fiber diameter: 50s–60s (30μ–23μ)
Staple length: 2–5 inches (50 mm–125 mm)
Found in: United Kingdom, Canada, United States

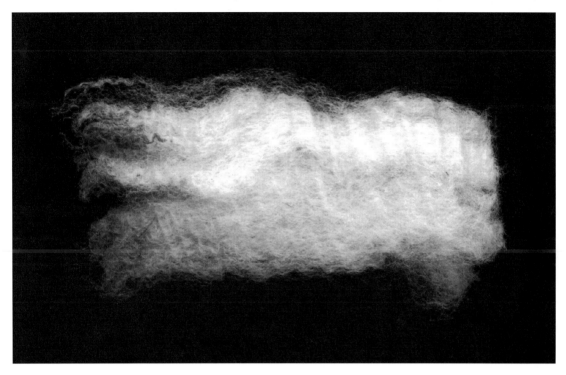

The Shropshire is another of the hardy British sheep which do well under rugged and varying climatic conditions. They are primarily a meat breed but produce a good fleece as well.

Shropshires are medium-sized with brown faces, ears, and legs. Their down-type wool is spongy and springy; the staples are large and rectangular with nearly flat tips.

Shropshire wool is used commercially in tweeds and flannel, hosiery, and hand-knitting yarns.

Fleece weight: 4½–6½ pounds (2 kg–3 kg)
Fiber diameter: 50s–58s (30µ–26µ)
Staple length: 3–4 inches (75 mm–100 mm)
Found in: United Kingdom, Australia, Canada, New Zealand, United States

In New Zealand during the 1950s, Dorset Down rams were crossed with Southdown ewes to produce this early-maturing breed particularly for the prime lamb export trade.

South Dorset Down sheep are medium-sized with brown faces and ears, and woolly legs. The wool, a typical down type, is full-handling and springy. Commercially, it is used for fabric, hosiery, and handknitting yarn.

Fleece weight: 4½–6½ pounds (2 kg–3 kg)
Fiber diameter: 56s–58s (28μ–25μ)
Staple length: 2–3 inches (50 mm–75 mm)
Found in: New Zealand

A Southdown/Hampshire cross, this breed was developed in New Zealand in the 1950s as a meat breed.

These sheep are medium-sized with dark brown faces, ears and legs.

The fleece is typical of down-type fleece: full-handling with large, fairly flat-tipped staples and little visible crimp. Individual fibers are well- but irregularly crimped. South Hampshire fleeces are free of black fibers.

The wool is used commercially to make handknitting yarns, hosiery, and flannels.

Fleece weight: 4½– 6½ pounds (2 kg–3 kg)
Fiber diameter: 56s–58s (28μ–25μ)
Staple length: 2–3 inches (50 mm–75 mm)
Found in: New Zealand

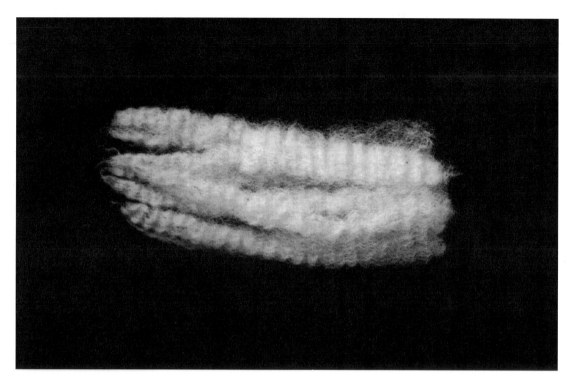

This Southdown × Suffolk sheep was bred in New Zealand to provide lean lamb.

South Suffolks are medium-sized sheep with dark brown faces, ears, and legs that are free of wool.

The springy, full-handling fleece is a typical down type, with large rectangular staples having nearly flat tips. Some colored fibers are found around the edges of the fleece. The wool is used mainly for hand-knitting yarns, hosiery, and apparel fabric.

Fleece weight: 4½–6½ pounds (2 kg–3 kg)
Fiber diameter: 56s–60s (28μ–23μ)
Staple length: 2–3 inches (50 mm–75 mm)
Found in: New Zealand

This largest of the Welsh mountain breeds is very hardy, thriving at high altitudes.

The faces and legs of South Wales Mountain sheep are white with tan markings; the faces and lower legs are free from wool. The ewes are polled, and the rams usually have horns.

South Wales Mountain fleece is very coarse and contains a high proportion of red and white kemp fibers. The staples are rectangular in shape with tapered tips. Although finer fleeces may be suitable for making upholstery fabrics or heavy tweeds, most fleeces will be most appropriate for carpet yarns.

Fleece weight: $2^{1}/_{4}$–$4^{1}/_{2}$ pounds (1 kg–2 kg)
Fiber diameter: 36s–40s and coarser (40+μ–36μ)
Staple length: 2–3 inches (50 mm–70 mm)
Found in: United Kingdom

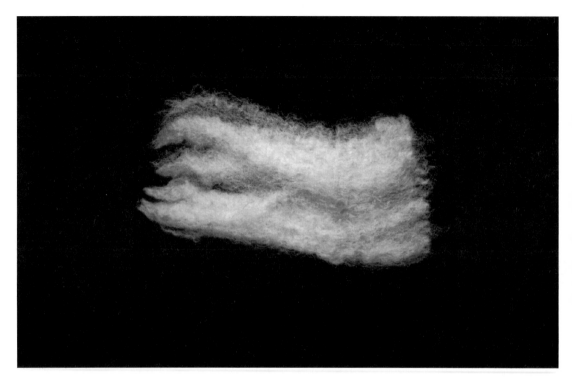

This is the original down sheep, which has grazed the rolling countryside (the Downs) of southern England for two centuries. The breed has figured in the evolution and development of all the other down breeds. It is bred primarily for its meat.

The Southdown, the smallest of all the down breeds, has short, woolly legs and a light brown face with a covering of short wool on the ears and upper face.

Southdowns provide the finest of the down wools—it is full-handling and spongy. The staples are indistinct in shape and crimp and have nearly flat tips.

Southdown wool is used commercially in knitwear blends, hosiery, dress fabrics, flannels, and light tweeds.

Fleece weight: 4½–6½ pounds (2 kg–3 kg)
Fiber diameter: 56s–60s (28μ–23μ)
Staple length: 2–3 inches (50 mm–75 mm)
Found in: England, Australia, France, New Zealand, United States

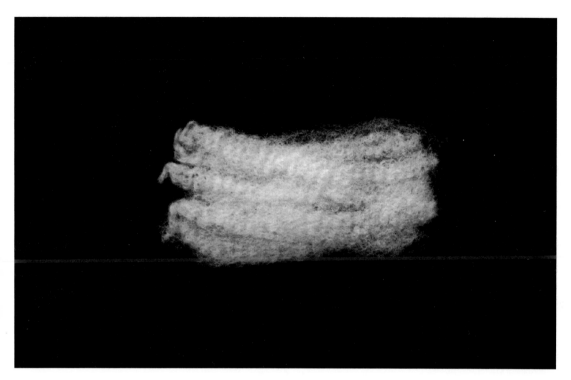

This is the most widespread breed in the United Kingdom, where it is used extensively as a sire for market lambs. It was developed in the nineteenth century from the crossing of Southdown rams with Norfolk Horn ewes.

Suffolks have large bodies, and their dark brown faces and legs are free of wool.

The short, down-type fleece has large, rectangular staples with nearly flat tips. It is full-handling and springy. Dark hairy fibers from the legs can often be found in the fleece.

Commercially, the wool is used for tweeds, flannels, hosiery, and handknitting yarns.

Fleece weight: 5–6½ pounds (2.5 kg–3 kg)
Fiber diameter: 56s–58s (28μ–26μ)
Staple length: 2–3 inches (75 mm–100 mm)
Found in: United States, Australia, New Zealand, elsewhere

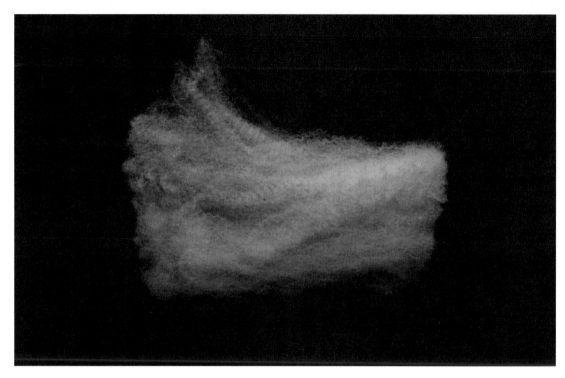

The Tunis is a very old breed of sheep believed to be descended from the fat-tailed sheep of biblical times. While the original fat-tailed Tunis sheep is still prevalent in the Near East, in America the breed has undergone some changes. With the introduction of Leicester and Southdown blood, the fat tail disappeared and the wool became finer and softer. Primarily a meat producer, Tunis is a hardy and long-lived breed.

Tunis lambs are born red or tan. As they grow, their fleece becomes white, but their clean faces and legs retain the original color.

The medium fleece is suitable for all preparation methods and is appropriate to use for a wide variety of knitted and woven fabrics.

Fleece weight: 7½–12 pounds (3.5 kg–5.5 kg)
Fiber diameter: 50s–58s (30μ–25μ)
Staple length: 3–5 inches (75 mm–125 mm)
Found in: United States

Originally from the hills of central Wales, Welsh Hill Speckled-Face sheep are larger than those of the Welsh Mountain breeds and have distinct white faces with black speckles on their noses, eyes, and ears. The ewes are polled; some rams have horns. Their faces and legs are free from wool. Welsh Hill Speckled-Face ewes are crossed with Blue-Faced Leicester rams to produce the Welsh Mule.

The fleece has rectangular staples with short tapered tips. The wool is resilient and hard-wearing, and well suited to making rugged outerwear, upholstery fabrics, and carpets.

Fleece weight: 3½–4½ pounds (1.5 kg–2 kg)

Fiber diameter: 48s–50s (33μ–29μ)

Staple length: 3–4¾ inches (70 mm–120 mm)

Found in: United Kingdom

This hardy and thrifty breed flourishes in the heavy rainfall and cold winds of the Welsh highlands. Welsh Mountain sheep are among the most common purebred sheep in Britain.

They are small sheep with light tan faces and legs that are free from wool. Only the rams have horns.

Welsh Mountain wool is surprisingly soft for a hill breed. It is resilient and lofty, and may contain kemp and black, gray, or red fibers, which make it attractive for use in tweeds and upholstery fabrics. Finer fleeces are suitable for making blankets, outer garment fabrics, and knitwear. Coarser fleeces can be used to make rugs.

Fleece weight: 3–4 pounds (1.2 kg–2 kg)
Fiber diameter: 36s–48s (40μ–32μ)
Staple length: 2–6 inches (50 mm–150 mm)
Found in: United Kingdom

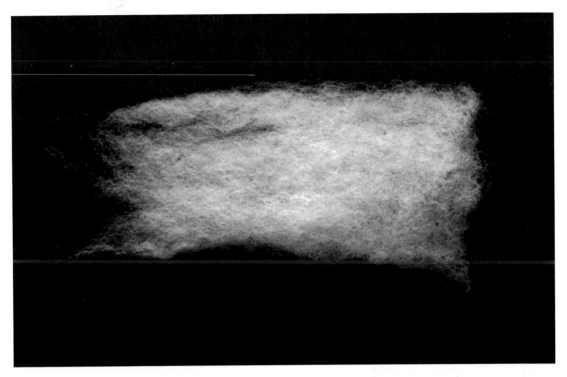

This very old Welsh breed, has (as its name suggests) a distinctive black-and-white striped "badger" face.

The sheep have black bellies and a broad black stripe running from the chin down the chest while the main body of the fleece varies from white to light tan. Their heads and legs are free of wool. The rams have dark horns. The most common color pattern, described above, is called *Torddu*; a less-common reverse coloring is known as *Torween*.

The staples are rectangular in shape with short tapered tips. The wool is medium to coarse and is suitable for making heavy, tweedlike outerwear, upholstery fabrics, and carpets.

Fleece weight: 3½–4½ pounds (1.5 kg–2 kg)
Fiber diameter: 46s–56s (34μ–26μ)
Staple length: 3–4 inches (70 mm–100 mm)
Found in: United Kingdom

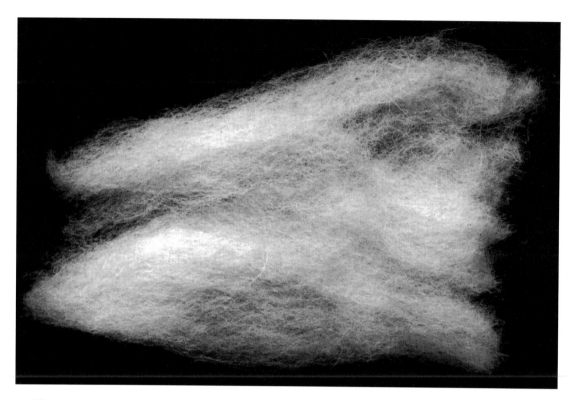

This is one of Britain's rare breeds. These large, hardy hill sheep have clean white faces and legs. Both sexes are horned.

With good loft and staple length, the wool is used commercially for handknitting yarns and blankets, while coarser fleeces are suitable for carpet yarns.

Fleece weight: 4½–6½ pounds (2 kg–3 kg)
Fiber diameter: 50s–54s (31μ–28μ)
Staple length: 4–6 inches (100 mm–150 mm)
Found in: United Kingdom

5
OTHER WOOLS

Spotted Jacob rams.
Photo courtesy of the Jacob Sheep Breeders Association.

DOUBLE-COATED SHEEP

Today's double-coated sheep have matured from an evolutionary split that took place before the development of modern breeds, such as Merino, Southdown, and Lincoln. They are on the whole very hardy breeds, at home in extreme environments and able to thrive on meager pastures. Their double-coated fleece no doubt contributes to their success under these conditions. The long, hairy outercoat intercepts and sheds rain and snow, while the short, fine undercoat forms an insulating layer next to the skin.

The fleeces are usually fairly open and airy with long triangular staples. The fine undercoat fills out the base of the staple, which then gradually tapers to a hairy tip. The outercoat usually has only a slight wave or no crimp at all, while the undercoat has a crimp in proportion to its fineness, but not as pronounced as the crimp in a single-layer fleece of similar fineness. Some breeds occur in a rich variety of natural colors; others are basically white, but the wool often contains kemp and colored fibers.

It is difficult to categorize double-coated fleeces by fiber diameter. Because both coats are usually processed together, the fleeces are usually graded simply as "coarse". While the undercoats in many cases are quite fine, it is the diameter of fibers in the outercoat which limits the use of the wool.

127

WASHING

Most double-coated fleeces contain little grease and will not require extensive washing. Treat the fleece gently if you eventually want to use both coats blended together. Too much handling may separate the coats. Although the long hair fibers do not felt readily by themselves, the undercoat does. When felting occurs, it usually affects the butt end of the staple and involves both fibers.

Naturally colored and dyed Icelandic fleece. The outer- and inner coats were prepared together on hand cards. Because the coarse outercoat may become harsh and wiry if tightly twisted, the yarn is very softly spun and plied.

PREPARATION

The two coats may be prepared and spun together or separated and used for different purposes. When prepared together, drum-carding or hand-carding keeps the fibers well mixed.

The coarseness of handle of its outercoat will usually dictate the best use for a fleece. Finer fleeces can be used to make garments and can be spun to preserve the same advantages that the sheep gets from the fleece: the outer hair will shed moisture while the soft inner coat provides warmth. Strong fleeces are excellent for use in rug and carpet making: the coarse hair provides durability, and the undercoat contributes loft and softness.

You can quickly separate the two types of fiber with a flick carder or single comb. Grasp a lock of fleece firmly by the long hairy tips as close as possible to the under-coat. Draw the flick carder or comb through the butt end of the lock to remove the undercoat, leaving the hair in your hand.

If the lock structure of the fleece has been disturbed, wool combs may be more effective in separating the two coats. Lash the locks onto the stationary comb by the butt. Make enough passes with the combs so that the undercoat is lodged in the teeth of the combs and the long hair is protruding. Grasp the long hair and pull it from the combs until only the undercoat remains.

The hair can be used to spin strong, hard-wearing, inelastic yarns for making rugs, braids, and warp. The undercoat by itself is usually soft and lofty, suitable for warm knitwear and soft woven fabrics. It may also be blended with other fibers.

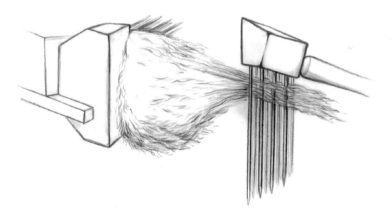

Wool combing with two combs is an effective method of separating double-coated fleeces when the outer- and undercoats have different staple lengths. Lash the fleece onto the stationery comb and make two to three passes of the combs. Draw the long outercoat from the stationery comb, leaving the shorter undercoat lodged in the tines.

A flick carder drawn through the butt end of the staple quickly separates the shorter undercoat from the long outercoat.

The Dalesbred is a rugged mountain breed, capable of thriving in the tough conditions and poor pastures of the Pennine Hills of northern England. It is very similar to the Swaledale in appearance and fleece type.

The Dalesbred can be distinguished from the Swaledale by a white mark above the nostrils on each side of the black face. Its legs are also black with white markings, and both face and legs are free of wool. Both sexes are horned. Dalesbred ewes are crossed with Teeswater or Wensleydale rams to produce the Masham crossbred.

The fleece is coarse and hairy with a fine undercoat. The hard-wearing and resilient wool is ideal for carpet yarns. Finer fleeces can also be used to make tough outer garments.

Fleece weight: 4½–6½ pounds (2 kg–3 kg)
Fiber diameter: 32s–40s (40+μ–36μ)
Staple length: 5–8 inches (130 mm–200 mm)
Found in: United Kingdom

The Herdwick is a native of the Lake District of England and is believed to have even earlier ties with Scandinavian breeds. It is one of Britain's hardiest sheep, able to thrive on the harsh mountain terrain without additional feeding. Herdwicks are also known for an extraordinary homing instinct, which allows the sheep to find their way home to the hill where they were born.

Herdwicks are born colored and gradually become lighter as they age. They have gray faces and legs and white ears. Rams may have horns while the ewes are polled.

The fleece is very coarse and contains brown and black pigmented fibers, long hairs, and kemp. The staples have long tapered tips and vary considerably in length.

The main commercial use of Herdwick wool is in carpets, but recently its unique mixture of fibers and natural colors has been used to good effect in specialty fabrics and knitwear. Handspinners can take advantage of the same characteristics to make attractive, hard-wearing carpet yarns and rugged, tweedlike outerwear.

Fleece weight: 3½–4½ pounds (1.5 kg–2 kg)
Fiber diameter: 40s and coarser (40+μ–36μ)
Staple length: 4–8 inches (100 mm–200 mm)
Found in: United Kingdom

The modern Icelandic breed evolved from the northern short-tailed sheep first brought to Iceland by Viking settlers more than a thousand years ago. These medium-sized, fine-boned sheep have no wool on their faces and legs. They have short, hairy tails and most have two horns; however, four-horned animals are not unusual. Although they are raised primarily for meat, their fleece has been valued by spinners for centuries.

Icelandic sheep come in a wide range of natural colors and markings, including white, black, gray, brown, and pied. The fleece is open and airy with very little grease. The coarse, long outercoat (called *tog*) is variable in diameter and character, while the inner coat (*thel*) is fine and soft.

Spun very softly, the two coats can be used together to make garments. The undercoat by itself is fine enough for use in next-to-the-skin wear or can be blended with other fine fibers. The outercoat by itself is suitable for floor coverings and hard-wearing knitted or woven fabrics.

Fleece weight: 5–6½ pounds (2.2 kg–3 kg)
Fiber diameter: outercoat, 50s–54s (31μ– 28μ); undercoat, 64s–70s (22μ–19μ)
Staple length: outer coat, 4–10 inches (100 mm–250 mm); undercoat, 2–3 inches (50 mm–75 mm)
Found in: Iceland, Canada, United States

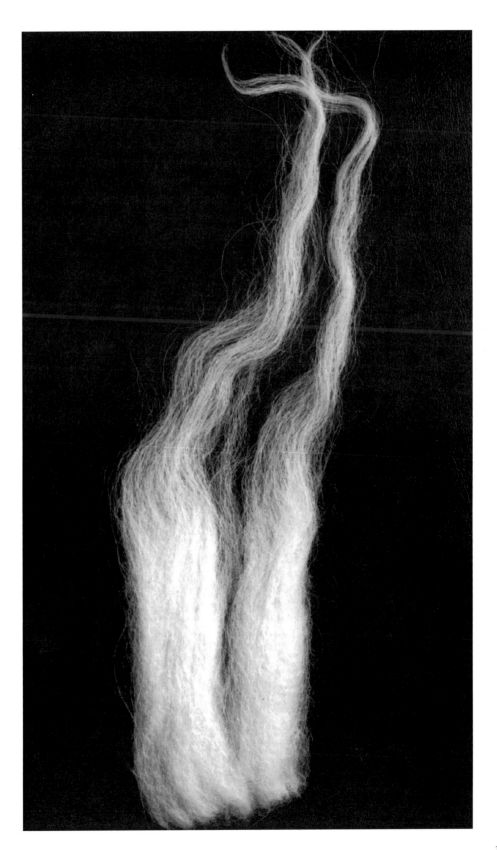

The Karakul is considered one of the oldest known breeds of sheep. It originated in the area of the former Soviet Union but has since been exported to many other parts of the world. The breed's nomadic, desert roots have made the Karakul a very hardy animal capable of surviving climatic extremes.

Karakuls have clean faces and legs, long, pendulous ears, and broad or fat tails. Most Karakuls are black, but other colors include brown, roan, gray, white, and pied. Lambs are born very dark and with a soft, curly, lustrous fleece often harvested as pelts known as Persian lamb.

When lambs reach the age of about four months, their double coats begin to develop; their fleeces become coarser and lighter with age. Fleeces are generally open and have very little grease. The fiber varies considerably in length, diameter, and style.

Used for centuries to make Oriental rugs and ethnic felts, double-coated Karakul wool is still valued for its strength and durability. Finer examples are soft enough for use in rugged outer garments while coarser fleeces are admirably suited to the traditional uses of carpets and upholstery fabrics.

Fleece weight: 5–10 pounds (2.2 kg–4.5 kg)
Fiber diameter: 50s and coarser (29+μ)
Staple length: 6–12 inches (150 mm–300 mm)
Found in: Central and eastern Asia, Canada, South Africa, Spain, United States, Romania

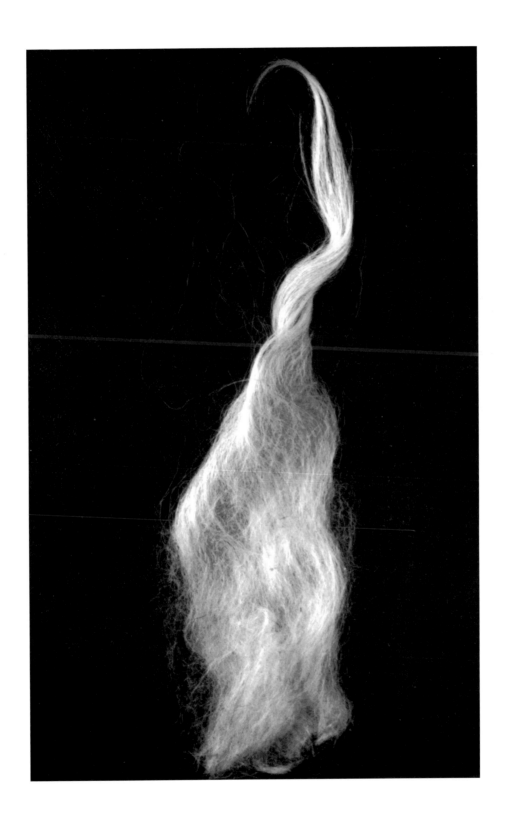

Churro sheep are natives of Spain and were initially brought to America by Spanish explorers as early as 1540, mainly as a source of food. They thrived in the arid ranges of the Southwest, and the Navajo living in that area were tending Churros by the late 1500s. By 1970, however, the Navajo-Churro was nearing extinction largely as a result of government efforts first to subdue the Navajo people and later to help them by introducing "improved" breeds of sheep that yielded finer wool and meatier carcasses. As a result of earlier cross breeding and the selective pressures of conditions in the American Southwest, modern Navajo-Churro sheep differ slightly from modern Spanish Churros, although they still closely resemble one another. Preservation efforts have built up numbers of the Navajo-Churro breed, and the wool is once again available to and used by American craftsmen.

The Navajo-Churro is a very hardy sheep with high resistance to internal parasites and foot rot. It is small-bodied, appears rough and shaggy, and is raised primarily for wool. The rams may be polled or may have two or four horns.

The fleece is open and double-coated with relatively little grease. The great variety of natural colors includes white, black, brown, tan, and gray. Fleeces may be spotted or have outer- and undercoats of different colors. The staples are long and tapered with pointed tips.

Limited quantities of the wool are commercially processed for traditional Navajo rug yarn.

Fleece weight: 5–7 pounds (2.2 kg–3.2 kg)
Fiber diameter: outercoat, 36s and coarser (38+μ); undercoat, 62s (22μ–23μ)
Staple length: outercoat, 4–14 inches (100 mm–350 mm); undercoat, 2–4 inches (50 mm–100 mm)
Found in: United States

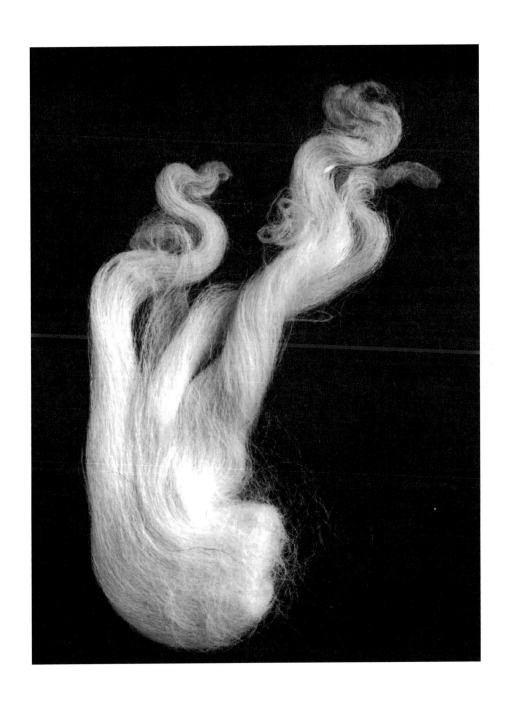

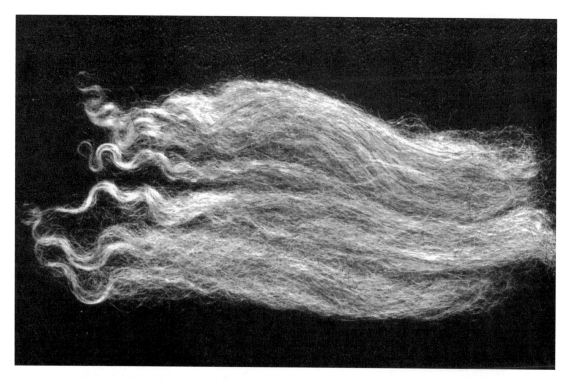

The Romanov is another breed from the northern short-tailed group. It originated in the area of the former Soviet Union in the late seventeenth century. Because Romanovs mature early, make excellent mothers, and are highly prolific, they are valued most for crossbreeding to produce high-performance ewes as well as crossbred market lambs.

Romanovs have the short, tapered tails characteristic of the group and are usually gray or black. Their faces and legs are black with white patches and are free of wool. The rams may have horns and a cape or mane of long, coarse hair about the neck.

The fleece is double-coated but differs from that of most other similar breeds in that, except for the mane in some rams, the coarse and fine coats are the same length. The fine coat makes up the bulk of the fleece. The major commercial use of the fleece in the past has been as pelts.

Fleece weight: 6½–13 pounds (3 kg–6 kg)
Fiber diameter: outercoat, 36s and coarser (150μ–40μ); undercoat, 64s–80s (22μ–16μ)
Staple length: 4–5 inches (100 mm–125 mm)
Found in: Central Asia, Canada, Europe, United States

The Rough Fell is a tough mountain breed well adapted to its home in northern England.

Rough Fells are similar in appearance and fleece type to the Scottish Blackface. Their faces and legs are free from wool and have black-and-white markings. Both sexes have horns.

The fleece is very coarse and hairy with an undercoat of finer fibers. In industry, the wool's toughness and resilience are valued for use in carpet yarns and as a mattress filling. Handspinners will find it most useful for making rug yarns.

Fleece weight: 5–8 pounds (2.2 kg–3.6 kg)
Fiber diameter: 40s and coarser (40+μ–36μ) (under- and outercoat together)
Staple length: 6–12 inches (150 mm–300 mm)
Found in: United Kingdom

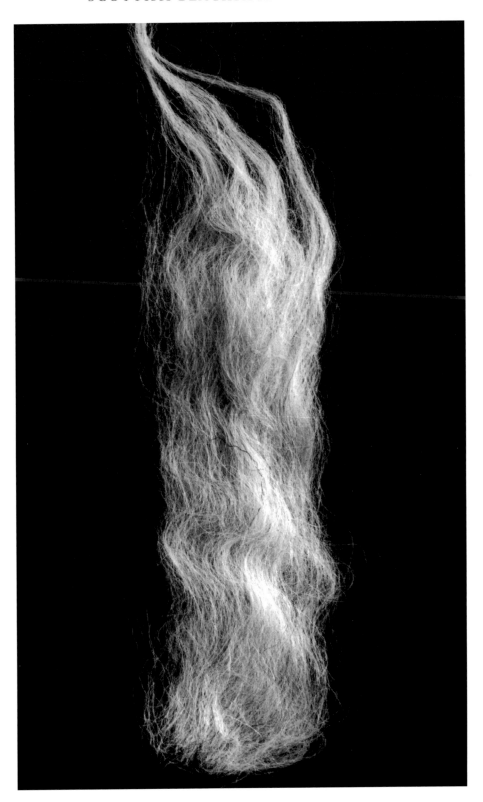

Known simply as Blackface in the United Kingdom, The Scottish Blackface is descended from the coarse-wooled sheep of medieval times; it evolved to graze the rugged mountain and hill country of Scotland and northern England.

These hardy sheep represent one of the most numerous and important breeds in Britain. They have black faces, clear of wool, with mottled white markings, and they sport black markings on white legs and feet. Both sexes have horns.

The fleece is long, very coarse, and hairy, with an undercoat of fine wool. The wool usually contains kemp and occasionally also some black fibers. It is often graded simply as "coarse" and not by count because of the wide range of fiber diameters in the staple.

Scottish Blackface wool is prized in the carpet industry and as a mattress filling, in which its excellent resilience is valuable. Some grades are also used to make Scottish and Irish tweeds. Handspinners will discover that the finer fleeces are suitable for the production of tough outerwear fabrics, and the coarser fiber makes sturdy rug and upholstery yarns.

Fleece weight: 4–6$\frac{1}{2}$ pounds (1.8 kg–3 kg)
Fiber diameter: 40s and coarser (40+μ–36μ)
Staple length: 6–12 inches (150 mm–300 mm)
Found in: United Kingdom, Canada, United States, Argentina, Italy

This old breed originated in western Norway, where it has been raised since medieval times.

The outercoat of a Spelsau fleece is long, lustrous, and very strong. The short, fine undercoat makes up about half of the fleece by weight, and it has its own soft sheen. Fleece colors include black, white, and a wide range of browns and grays.

Both coats of finer fleeces can be used together for woven or knitted outer garments. The inner coat is soft and silky and makes soft, draping fabrics. The outercoat is suitable for floor coverings and hard-wearing knitted or woven fabrics.

Fleece weight: 5–6½ pounds (2.2 kg–3 kg)
Fiber diameter: outercoat, 40s–46s (40μ–37μ); undercoat, 64s–70s (22μ–19μ)
Staple length: outercoat, 5–7 inches (130 mm–180 mm); undercoat, 2–2½ inches (50 mm–65 mm)
Found in: Norway

The Swaledale is a very hardy British mountain breed, well adapted to the harsh environment of the Yorkshire moors, the Pennine Hills, and the Lake District, where it thrives. Swaledale ewes crossed with a Blue-Faced Leicester ram produce the very popular Mule crossbred.

Swaledales have dark faces with light gray noses. Their legs are mottled dark gray. Their faces and legs are free from wool, and both sexes are horned.

The fleece is long and hairy with a fine, dense undercoat that gives the staples the long tapered form typical of mountain breeds. The wool is also likely to contain kemp and black fibers.

Finer grades can be used for tough outerwear fabrics, but the bulk of Swaledale wool will be most suitable for spinning rug and carpet yarns.

Fleece weight: $3^{1}/_{2}$–$6^{1}/_{2}$ pounds (1.5 kg–3 kg)
Fiber diameter: 30s–40s ($40+\mu$–36μ) (under- and outercoat together)
Staple length: 4–8 inches (100 mm–200 mm)
Found in: United Kingdom

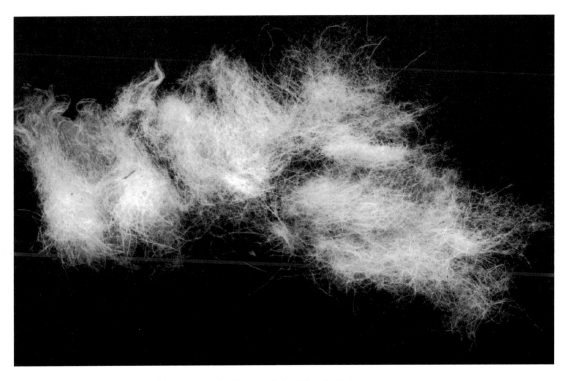

Short, bristly fleece of the Katahdin hair sheep.

Hair sheep are generally raised exclusively for their meat. Some of the better-known breeds are Barbados, Barbados Blackbelly, Katahdin, Persian Blackhead, Saint Croix, West African, and Wiltshire Horn. Many of these breeds originated in tropical and subtropical regions of the world, where wool is of little value but the ability to thrive in warm temperatures is essential.

The "fleece" of these animals is of no commercial value, and in most cases is simply shed each year. This makes these sheep easy to care for and eliminates shearing and wool-handling costs.

The wool is usually very short, coarse, and hairy with no clearly defined staple or crimp. Its only value to handspinners may be as a blend with other fleeces to produce a hairy, tweedlike texture.

PRIMITIVE AND FERAL SHEEP

Primitive sheep represent some of the intermediate stages in the evolution of modern breeds from the first domesticated sheep. They survived where other breeds either died out or were modified to fill modern demands. Soay sheep are thought to be decended from Stone Age domestic sheep and the North Ronaldsay, also known as Red Orkney, may be the remnants of Iron Age domestic sheep.

Feral sheep are also a source of primitive traits. These sheep are domesticated animals that have been released or escaped and in response to isolation and the selective pressures of their environment have over time acquired primitive fleece characteristics once again.

The features that distinguish primitive breeds from the modern breeds are a short, fine, woolly coat mixed with hair or kemp, a predominance of colored fleeces, and a tendency to molt annually. Some of these sheep have found a niche in the specialty wool industry, where their wool has curiosity value and the natural colors can be used to good advantage.

From the handspinner's point of view, these sheep offer interesting alternatives. Bear in mind that some are also rare breeds and their numbers are small. If raised solely because they are rare, scant attention may be paid to producing a high-quality fleece. As a result, fleeces of a given breed can vary greatly. Take heart, however: after preservation efforts have ensured the survival of a breed, the production of good fleeces may then be addressed.

This rare breed now survives mostly as a feral flock on its native island of Boreray, west of the Hebrides. It is thought to be the result of crossing a very early variety of Scottish Blackface with either the Soay or the Scottish Dunface.

Borerays are very small sheep: the ewes weigh about 60 pounds (27 kg). They have black or tan faces and legs; fleece colors include white, tan, and dark brown. Both sexes have horns.

The fleece is coarse and suitable for the production of heavy outerwear fabrics and rugs.

Originating on the islands off the west coast of Scotland, these small sheep were once common throughout Scotland but are now rare.

Their faces and legs are black and free from wool. Both sexes are usually horned, with two, four, or occasionally six horns. The fleece is black or dark brown, contains hair and kemp, and usually becomes lighter as the sheep ages. Attractive because of its natural color, the wool is suitable for knitted outerwear.

Fleece weight: 3½–5 pounds (1.5 kg–2.2 kg)
Fiber diameter: 44s–50s (36μ–29μ)
Staple length: 2–6 inches (50 mm–150 mm)
Found in: United Kingdom

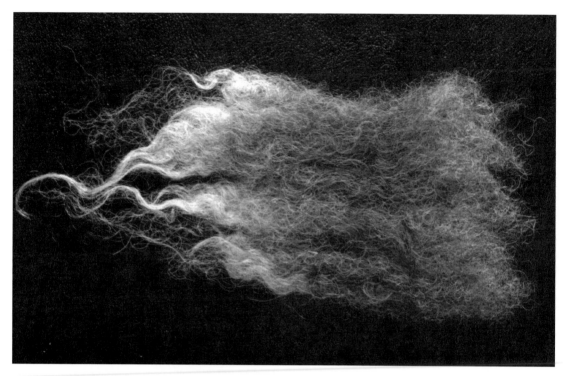

Manx Loghtans are descended from primitive sheep of Scotland and the islands off Britain. Most of these sheep are now found on the Isle of Man.

They are small, reddish brown sheep with clean faces and legs. Both sexes may have two, four, or six horns.

The fleece is open and airy. The staples have short tapered tips, moderate crimp, and almost no luster. Its natural reddish bown color makes this a particularly attractive wool for knitted or woven outerwear.

Fleece weight: $3\frac{1}{2}$–$4\frac{1}{2}$ pounds (1.5 kg–2 kg)
Fiber diameter: 46s–54s (32μ–28μ)
Staple length: $2\frac{1}{2}$–4 inches (70 mm–100 mm)
Found in: United Kingdom

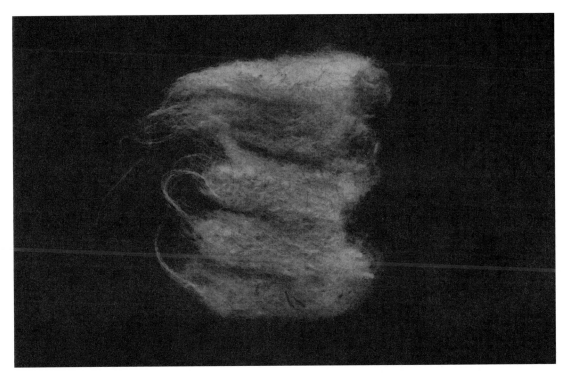

This tough, hardy breed is well adapted to its native home, the Orkney Islands northeast of Scotland. It is considered to be characteristic of Iron Age domestic sheep and to represent the ancestral stock from which the modern Shetland breed evolved.

These small, fine-boned animals have short tails and come in a variety of colors, including gray, white, black, and brown. Although sometimes contaminated with sand if the sheep have been grazing at the seashore, the fleece is good quality and used for specialty knitted garments.

Fleece weight: 3½–5½ pounds (1.5 kg–2.5 kg)
Fiber diameter: 50s–56s (31μ–26μ)
Staple length: 1½–3 inches (40 mm–80 mm)
Found in: United Kingdom

These are the feral descendants of sheep brought to the Saint Kilda Islands, which lie about forty miles west of the Hebrides. The Soay are thought to be very similar to the European domestic sheep of the Bronze Age.

Soays are brown with white bellies, and their fleeces are highly variable: some are woolly and others are more hairy. Both ewes and rams have horns, and the fleece is molted every year.

When spun, the variation in color and the mix of wool and hair fibers in the fleece make an attractive tweed yarn suitable for outerwear.

Fleece weight: 3½–5 pounds (1.5 kg–2.2 kg)
Fiber diameter: 44s–50s (36μ–29μ)
Staple length: 2–4 inches (50 mm–100 mm)
Found in: United Kingdom

JACOB

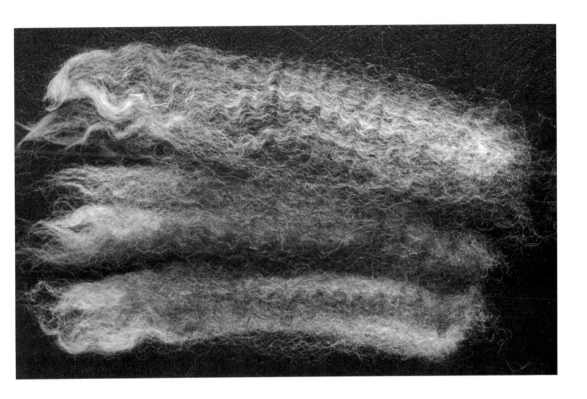

The exact geographical and genetic origin of the Jacob breed is uncertain, but they may have come first from the Middle East, spent some time in Spain, and finally arrived in Britain in the sixteenth century. With their multiple horns and attractively colored fleeces, most Jacobs were kept in English parks as ornamental animals. Jacobs are able to thrive on a small amount of feed. They make excellent mothers, and produce good meat in addition to their distinctive fleece.

These medium-sized sheep have black-and-white patched fleeces. The black gradually fades to brown as the sheep ages. The color pattern and the relative amounts of black and white vary considerably among individual sheep. The sheep have two, four, and sometimes six horns.

The fleece is open, lofty, and semilustrous, and usually has a silky handle. The staples are indistinct, with short pointed tips and moderately developed crimp. Some fleeces may contain kemp fibers or show a difference in character between the white and colored portions.

Most Jacob wool is used to produce specialty wool fabrics and knitwear, or for handspinning. It is suitable for all preparation methods and makes excellent outerwear and blankets.

Fleece weight: 4–5½ pounds (2 kg–2.5 kg)
Fiber diameter: 48s–56s (33μ–26μ)
Staple length: 3–6 inches (80 mm–150 mm)
Found in: United Kingdom, Canada, United States

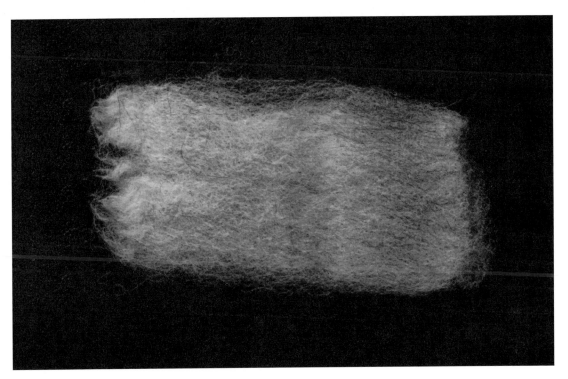

This unusual breed was developed in California, starting in 1971 with a cross of Barbados and American-bred Tunis which was then recrossed to Tunis. (The Barbados is a meat breed, developed in Texas from Barbados Blackbelly with the addition of some American Rambouillet.) The original intent was to produce a meat breed that needed no shearing. However, the further crossing with Tunis resulted in a substantial fleece comprising a combination of wool and red-brown hair fibers, which gives the fleece a distinctive pink-beige color.

California Red sheep are fine-boned, good-natured, hardy, and adaptable. The ewes are very easy lambers, and both sexes are polled. The fleece has blocky staples with short, slightly tapered tips. The wool has very little luster and a well-developed fine, irregular crimp, which gives it good loft. The colored hair fibers are coarser and shorter than the wool, and have only a suggestion of the irregular crimp. The hair tends to separate from the wool during preparation. Hand-carding and drum-carding preserve the mix of fibers whereas flick-carding and combing tend to separate the hair from the wool.

Only a relatively small number of California Red sheep exist, and because they are principally a meat breed, there is no commercial market for the wool as yet. The combination of hair and wool fibers makes for warm, rugged, tweedlike fabrics and sweaters.

Fleece weight: 5–7 pounds (2.2 kg–3.2 kg)
Fiber diameter: 50s–54s (31μ–28μ)
Staple length: 3–4 inches (75 mm–100 mm)
Found in: United States

Sometimes mistaken for the Jacob breed, Harlequin or spotted sheep constitute a color pattern rather than a distinct breed. Many breeds produce the occasional spotted sheep. These animals are interbred and selected in an attempt to fix the spotted color pattern. The sheep are frequently very small—often the result of interbreeding—with brown-and-white patched and/or spotted fleeces. Because many different breeds may contribute to the flock, fleece characteristics can be extremely variable.

6
BLACK AND COLORED WOOLS

Soay ram about to start shedding its fleece.
Photograph by N.F. Stone, courtesy of the Rare Breeds Survival Trust, Warwickshire, U.K.

The expression "the black sheep of the family" is often used to describe a relative who in some major or minor way has brought dishonor to the clan. Its origin can probably be traced back to the book of Genesis, in which there is reference to Jacob culling the flocks of Laban, removing all the brown, spotted, and speckled stock. (Whereas Laban considered these sheep to be undesirable, Jacob built his fortune on them.)

Fine-wooled sheep were bred in ancient Greece. These highly prized animals were well-tended and covered with cloth or skins to keep the wool soft and beautiful. Breeders in Asia Minor lavished the same care on their flocks. The fine black fleeces of Laodicea were much sought after and brought great wealth to their producers.

Over the years, the popularity of colored fleece has waxed and waned. The black sheep remained the undesirable element on the sheep farm from the end of the nineteenth century until the 1950s, when a resurgence of interest in the ancient crafts of handspinning and weaving resulted in some demand for black and colored fleece. Later, fashion designers, too, sought the rich, earthy colors of natural-colored fleece as a basis for their color palette.

161

Industry still classes color in fleece as a fault, and the term "black wool" is often used to describe any fiber that is not white. Recently, however, farmers in a number of sheep-producing countries have formed associations whose aim is to produce high-quality natural-colored fleece mainly for handcraft use. Instead of culling "black" sheep from their flocks, breeders selectively breed and carefully tend colored individuals to produce beautiful fleece of all types, from fine, soft Merino to strong, lustrous longwools.

Sheep farmers who maintain white flocks breed for different end results. Some are wool producers, some are meat producers, and some raise sires or ewes for producing crossbred market lambs. Like any grower of high-quality fleece, the successful breeder of natural-colored sheep is a specialist wool producer with a strong feeling for his animals and a genuine interest in the beauty of the fiber that they yield. These days, the shepherd with a colored flock is dependent upon and closely allied with the needs of handspinners and other craftspersons working in wool.

THE COLOR IN THE FLEECE

The color in naturally colored fleeces comes from small granules of *melanin*, the same pigment that influences the skin and hair coloring of human beings. There are two biochemically different types of the melanin pigment that make possible the full spectrum of naturally colored fleeces. Eumelanin is responsible for black and all shades of gray from charcoal to pale moonlight silver, and also responsible for the less common dark chocolate brown (often called moorit) and all the paler shades

through caramel to café au lait. Generally, a sheep may possess black or brown eumelanin but not both. The pale shades of black and brown are brought about either by a mixture of white fibers with colored fibers or by clumped distribution of pigment in the fiber.

The second pigment, pheomelanin, is responsible for red and tan coloring which usually shows only in hair and kemp fibers or in the outercoats of sheep that have them. This coloring is much rarer in domestic sheep than black or brown but shows up in some very old breeds that have hairy coats and some hair sheep and breeds that include red hair-sheep blood. Some examples are Karakul, Barbados Blackbelly, and the face and leg hair of the Tunis.

The depth of color in a fleece changes over the sheep's lifetime just as our hair turns gray as we age.

USING COLORED FLEECE

How can these well-bred fleeces be used to the best advantage? There are many ways to bring out the innate beauty of natural-colored fleeces. They can be used just as they come from the sheep's back, of course. In some fleeces, the color is even over most of the fleece, but in others, it is quite variable. The basic options are these:

- Using the wool "just as it comes" produces a sort of space-dyed effect.
- Sorting the color variations within a fleece and using these in various combinations (for instance, from dark to light or light to dark).
- Selecting two or more distinct shades gives you the option of making patterned knitwear or subtly checked woven fabrics.

162

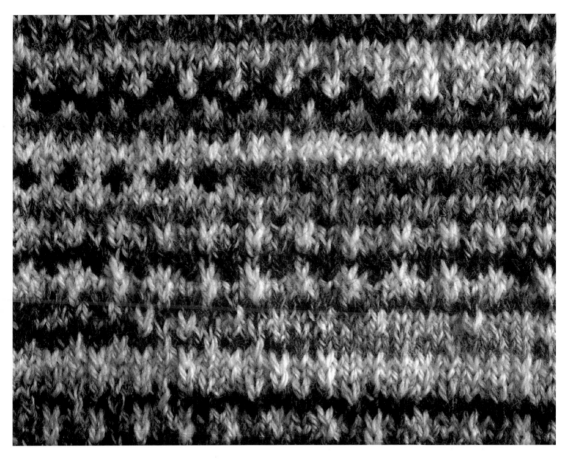

Locks of Jacob fleece were flick-carded and randomly selected for spinning. Navajo-plying preserves the color differentiation and a slipped stitch knitting pattern worked with a single strand of yarn creates a multicolored-like design.

- Spinning random yarn from the different color groupings and plying with singles of just one color produces skeins of different but related ragg-type yarns.
- Spinning lengths of random colors and then Navajo-plying (see page 208) yields yarn with lengths of solid color.

There are hosts of other ways of producing attractive visual effects from natural-colored wool. If you particularly want a "one-color" effect but your colored fleece has a variety of different shades, the wool can be blended thoroughly either on a drum carder or by your favorite carding company. The way in which you use your wool is all a matter of taste and requirement, but beware of overblending. Gray fleeces especially may appear lifeless if blended to complete homogeneity.

Overdyeing natural-colored fleece can provide a wealth of subtle and glorious tones. If you dye several shades of wool at the same time in one dyepot—from white to mid- or dark gray—you will achieve a dynamic monochromatic range of compatibly colored fibers. This can be quite a boon to the busy fiber worker!

If you haven't tried overdyeing, you have a treat in store. It is fun and it is fruitful. For example, it is difficult to obtain a really good black when dyeing white fleece, but overdye a very dark natural-colored fleece with blue or red and see what happens.

White sheep are just black sheep in white pajamas.

—Stefan Adalsteinsson, Icelandic geneticist

SELECTING COLORED FLEECE

Colored sheep are found within every breed and wool type in the world. Although most breeders are selecting from and for white sheep, and have been doing so for generations, every now and then a colored sheep appears in the flock. If these sheep are interbred, their offspring will also be colored. In several breeds (for example, Soay and Karakul), the wool is almost always colored, and a white animal is the exception.

The same criteria for length, soundness, and so forth, should be used for selecting all wool, white or colored (see pages 169–172). When examining a dark fleece, however, pay particular attention to the tips, which can be very brittle. These should be snipped off before spinning to avoid breakage of the fiber within the yarn. This treatment can be given to any undesirable tips such as discolored ones.

On the other hand, some gray fleeces have sound, attractive, creamy tips which you may want to highlight. To do so, spin the staple from the tip rather than the cut end so that the creamy tips stay on the outside of the yarn instead of being hidden in its core.

Examine light-colored fleece especially well for yellowing. This is not readily visible on a cursory inspection, but it can be quite noticeable in the skein or finished garment.

You may come across a dark fleece with one or more white bands through the staples. This effect looks magnificent, and the mind races on to thoughts of how it can be excitingly exploited, but more often than not the fibers will be tender at the bands. Check them. If they are weak, don't buy the whole fleece; instead, ask for a sample so that you can look at it when you need a lift in spirits. It is easy to be carried away by the beauty of fleece, and it is very true that if you "select your fleece in haste" you will "repent at leisure"!

Handspinners are sometimes asked to pay higher prices for hand-reared colored fleece. Regrettably, some breeders feel that the price should be high simply *because* the sheep are hand-reared. If the fleece is not of superior quality, this factor alone counts for nothing. However, if the wool quality is outstanding due to the individual and wise tending, a higher price is justified and you will get good value for your money.

When faced with a premium price tag, bear in mind the tender loving care with which these sheep may have been raised (some fleeces even come labeled with the names of the sheep from which they were shorn). The beautiful fleeces that an experienced shepherd can produce will be available only while there is a market for them, so make good use of the bounty of their harvest.

WASHING AND PREPARATION

It is not the color of the fleece that will influence your choice of washing and preparation methods, but the type of wool. Select the appropriate methods for your colored fleece from the fine-wool, long-wool, or down-wool chapters. Colored fleece does gradually fade with exposure to light but always leaves you with gentle, muted tones.

7
SELECTING, SORTING, AND STORING FLEECE

DESIGN CRITERIA

Apart from its use in felt making and specific decorative purposes, wool is generally spun into yarn before it is used. Yarn itself is not an end product and it is the use for which a yarn is intended that will influence the choice of fleece. In other words, the fleece needs to be selected to fit the design criteria for the job at hand.

If the above heading causes an immediate body stiffening, a glazed-over brain, and/or a burning desire to move on to the next chapter, relax. The phrase is shorthand for the process of thinking about what you are going to make and how you will make it. This mental exercise takes only a few minutes and will allow you to set about your work with confidence and direction.

For example, imagine that you want to spin a yarn and make a knitted sweater for a child. What qualities do you need in the finished garment? Those that immediately spring to mind are:

Comfort—No child will happily wear anything that is uncomfortable.
Durability—Life in the playground is pretty tough!
Washability—Few children stay clean.
Visual impact—This quality is desirable for any garment.

To achieve these qualities, several stages of production need to be addressed:
Choice of Fleece
Preparation of Fleece
Design of Yarn
Quality of Fabric
Design of Finished Piece—colors, decoration, pattern or stitch.

The first three items on the list come within the scope of this book. Let's look at them objectively.

CHOICE OF FLEECE

A strong, harsh fleece will produce a rough and prickly yarn that is sure to get a thumbs-down rating from anyone who has to wear it, not only children. On the other hand, a very fine, soft fleece will require a great deal of work to produce a yarn that is durable and washable. It can be done, of course, but you may not be willing to invest the effort for a garment that will receive such hard use. A fleece that feels comfortable to the touch and is not too fine would seem to be the ideal choice.

PREPARATION OF FLEECE

Worsted-type yarn (see page 18) will wear much better than woolen yarn (see page 19). This further narrows the choice in our example to a fleece of good length that can be combed (with a single comb or with wool combs) or flick-carded.

Fleece characteristics may vary considerably within a breed.

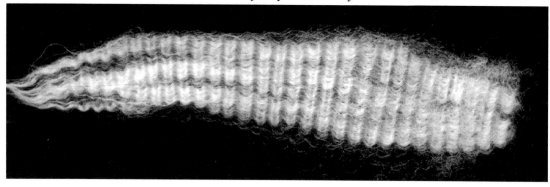

Fine Romney.

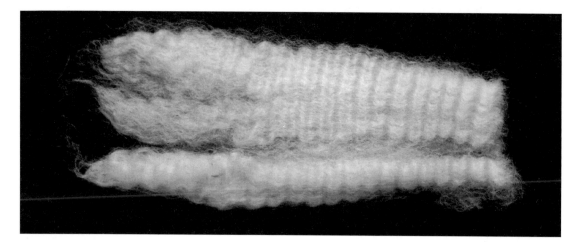

Medium Romney.

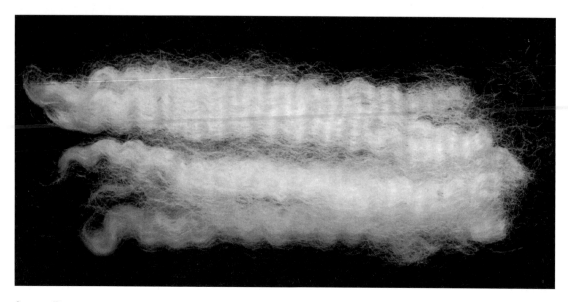

Strong Romney.

DESIGN OF YARN

A lightly spun yarn will be vulnerable to the rigors of rough-and-tumble play. A soft yarn will quickly wear through if it has to endure being tied around the neck or waist, dumped on the ground for use as a cushion, dragged along the concrete, and used as a football. Instead, for our example, we need a smooth, fairly firmly spun yarn.

The indignities that the garment can be expected to suffer make frequent washing a safe bet. In addition to avoiding a fleece that felts readily, the quality of the knitting will affect washability. Too firm a fabric will tend to felt whereas fabric that is too flimsy will not keep its shape and will snag easily.

Decision Time! Of the many "correct" breed wools that would meet our criteria, we might suggest Romney, Perendale or Gromark, in each case choosing a fleece on the finer end of their breed's range, or a Corriedale or New Zealand Halfbred, on the stronger end of their breed's scale. We might also consider a Montadale, Finnish Landrace or a down/finewool or down/longwool cross.

If you look back through this section, you will see that in working through the practical aspects of the design criteria, you have identified not only the fleece but also the preparation, spinning, and finishing techniques that will turn that fleece into a successful finished garment.

SELECTING FOR QUALITY

Time spent in selecting fleece both for suitability of purpose and for quality is never wasted. It is your best investment for good results.

You have worked through the design criteria for your project and are now ready to purchase your fleece. How do you make your selection to ensure that you are getting quality fiber? What do you look for?

Always tip the fleece from the bag and examine it carefully, without disturbing the arrangement of the locks—in many cases, the fleece will have been rolled to preserve its shape as it left the animal, and this alignment can be an advantage to the spinner who later sorts the wool for use.

There is no substitute for putting your hands into a fleece and really feeling the fiber. The breed name gives an indication of a fleece's characteristics but only as a range of possibilities within that type. An individual fleece will fall within the extremes of the range, but where, exactly? Variations occur even within a fleece, which is why many handspinners prefer hogget or yearling (first-year) fleeces, in which the variation within the fleece is much less than in an older animal.

A *shorn hogget*, or yearling fleece comes from a sheep aged between seven and eighteen months; this sheep was shorn once before as a lamb, but this is its first full fleece. The wool is very consistent and will require less sorting than a fleece from an older animal, because the amount and quality of wool change as a sheep ages. The locks of a *woolly hogget*, which has missed the initial lamb shearing, have characteristic short, tightly curled corkscrew tips which are the remnants of the birth coat.

Merino wool tends to be more consistent in quality throughout the whole fleece than other breeds, even as the animal matures, so there is not such a radical difference between a Merino hogget fleece and that of an older animal. Recently, some breeders sensitive to the needs of handspinners have begun to select for animals in other breeds with more uniform wool throughout the fleece.

Only by handling and checking can you ensure that a given fleece will fulfill your needs. All breeds and wool types will vary according to the particular strain, the geographical situation in which they were raised, climatic conditions and feed supply, and the quality of farm management practiced by the grower.

Remember the variety in human hair? Take any sheep breed—say, Romney. There are fine Romneys, medium Romneys and strong (or coarse) Romneys. A fine Romney could be perfect for your winter sweater but a strong one would probably be most unsuitable—hair shirt material! That same strong Romney would make great carpet yarn, though. Before you shop, consider the characteristics that your fleece will need to have so that you can achieve the results you want. You are likely to get better service from your supplier if she or he can get a good indication of the type of fleece you are seeking.

Here we are at the breeder's, the farm or ranch, the craft shop, or wherever you buy your fleece. You are looking at several fleeces in the range you have previously decided could be suitable. Below is a checklist for ensuring that your money is spent wisely.

- Handle and staple definition
- Soundness or strength
- Length
- Crimp
- Color
- Vegetable matter

HANDLE

When selecting a fleece for garments, whether knitted, crocheted, or woven, the handle of that fleece or how it feels to the touch, is critical. There is no pleasure in wearing an itchy garment. We are looking for protection, comfort, and beauty in our garments. The handle should be appropriate for its intended use.

How soft a fleece feels is related to the fineness of the wool fiber. The finer the fleece, the softer it feels. Conversely, the coarser or stronger the fleece, the harsher it feels.

The fleece should fall freely, with adjacent locks loosely connected but moving independently. The fleece should not feel stiff. The natural groupings or locks of fibers, called staples, should separate easily. Avoid fleece which is matted (cotted) requiring that you wrench the staples apart. In addition to the problem of time and effort required to separate the staples, pulling mats apart may break the fibers; there is also often a permanent yellow stain, also called canary stain (see page 174), associated with cotting.

SOUNDNESS AND STRENGTH

Many wool graders use the following method to test for strength. Hold a single staple firmly and straight, between the thumb and index finger of each hand. With your middle finger, flick the staple across its midsection. If the fleece is sound, you should hear a good, healthy ping. If (like one of the authors) you are unable to master this cunning technique, instead grasp each end of a staple in either hand and quickly move the hands closer to each other, then away, listening for that same healthy ping.

A flick carder (see page 189) can help determine suitability in terms of strength. Flick-card a couple of staples at both the cut and the tip ends, then look at the flick carder and see what (if any) fleece has remained in the teeth. Make your own judgment as to whether the waste is acceptable or not.

Quite often, a break in the fleece (caused by poor health or by lambing or feeding problems) is easily seen on inspection of the staple. A break is not a parting of the fibers but an interruption in the growth pattern of the fiber. It can often be seen as a change in the crimp pattern. A colored fleece may show a color change at the point of weakness. If in doubt, hold a staple up to your ear. Grasp it firmly by each end and pull. If you hear a crackling sound, you are in trouble—or rather the sheep was, and you had best look at other fleeces.

A very slight weakening of the fiber may have no effect on your project at all. If the break is near the tip or the butt (the end shorn from the fleece), it can be easily removed, still leaving a good length of sound wool. (If you are spinning superfine fleece, you'll probably want to remove the tip anyway to ensure a smooth, even yarn without any discoloration.) You may not consider the time spent removing the broken fiber ends to be worthwhile; however, in some cases you may have a very good reason for doing so: perhaps the type or color of fleece is particularly appealing and unavailable elsewhere.

LENGTH

The staples should be consistent in length from the butt to the tip. Check the tips. Staples from different breed types have differently shaped tips. For instance, Merino fleece has flat-tipped staples as do those of the down breeds. Tips of the staples of other breeds are more V-shaped.

Avoid excessively pointed, discolored, or dry tips. They are likely to be harsh and therefore undesirable for garment use; a fleece with these characteristics is referred to as *tippy*. Damaged tips are also prone to breaking off during preparation. The preceding strength test may not detect brittle tips, but the visual clues mentioned will alert you to the possibility.

Because of the natural waviness or curl of the wool fibers (called crimp), the average fiber length will be greater than the staple length. When we look at the general fleece characteristics of the different breeds, there is a loose correlation between the fineness of the wool and the length of the staple. Although there are exceptions, generally, the finer the fiber, the shorter the staple. The staple length of wool from a particular breed will usually fall into a certain range.

CRIMP

Each breed or type of sheep grows fleece with a characteristic crimp pattern. Regardless of the appropriate pattern for the breed, the crimp should be consistent along the full length of the staple. Although it is sometimes suggested that this factor is less important than once believed, the crimp can give the handspinner clues about the most appropriate yarn diameter to be spun from a particular fleece. If a fine yarn is desired, look for a fine fleece with about twelve crimps to the inch (2.5 cm). A strong fleece with two or three crimps to the inch (2.5 cm) *can* be spun into a fine yarn, but the yarn will be harsh and stringy. A fine fleece *can* be successfully spun into a soft, bulky yarn, but because so little twist is required, the fibers may be insufficiently twisted to resist fluffing and felting during washing.

When trying to decide what weight of yarn would be appropriate to spin from a particular fleece, start with a sample of a yarn that when plied will fit neatly into the crimp pattern of the fleece.

You can do some initial sampling right on the spot before you buy. Take a staple of the fleece you are considering. From the butt end, draft out a few fibers for a distance

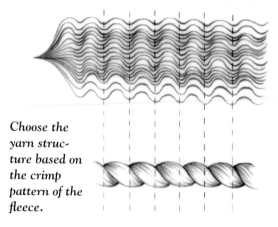

Choose the yarn structure based on the crimp pattern of the fleece.

less than the length of the staple; twist these fibers with your fingers. Keep on drafting and twisting, a few fibers at a time, until the yarn is 6 to 8 inches (15 to 20 cm) long. Fold the twisted yarn double and let it wrap around itself and you have a miniature sample of spun and plied yarn. Try finger-twisting the same fleece into several different weights of yarn. Look carefully at the samples and decide which (if any) will be suitable for the purpose you have in mind.

Wool should be white or, in the case of a colored fleece, clear. The whitest and brightest wool is Merino, followed by that of the other fine-wool breeds, through to the wool of the long-wool breeds, which may look light cream in color. Watch out for unscourable stains, the most common of which is canary stain (see page 176). If in doubt about whether a stain is permanent, run two or three staples under some running water and see if the odd color disappears. There will usually be a tap, even if only cold water, close at hand. If the wool does not wash out white, look for another fleece unless your plans call for dyeing or another type of camouflage.

VEGETABLE MATTER

This little extra, for which you are paying full fleece rates, is not wanted in a garment and if present in quantity can require a great deal of time and effort to remove. Accumulated mud and dirt are also to be avoided. There will always be some vegetation and dust present, but avoid a fleece showing heavy contamination. Very fine wool fleeces, particularly those of Merino strains (unless the sheep have been coated), will usually have dirty tips, which are removed before spinning. Burs can be real bugbears to remove and give some nasty jabs. Speaking of jabs, be sure to keep your tetanus shots up to date. Although the risk is small, it is better to be safe than sorry.

SORTING A FLEECE

Why should you sort a fleece? Believe it or not, a single sheep may have as many as fourteen different types of wool covering it, depending on the breed, the individual, and its age. Some of these portions are separated out in the shearing shed in a process called skirting and are seldom seen when fleece is purchased. Skirting generally removes bellies, necks, eye pieces, topknots, and stained areas around the outside of the fleece.

You are still left with a lot of variety. Problems that you can prevent by careful sorting include uneven yarn, different rates of shrinkage, and uneven results from dyeing (different parts of the fleece may absorb dye at differing rates).

Spread an old sheet out on the floor or grass. Tip your new purchase onto it and spread it out with the tips uppermost, trying to keep it as near to its original "sheep" shape as possible. This will be quite easy if the fleece has been rolled into a compact parcel in the shearing shed. If it hasn't, do the best you can. Use natural dividing lines when separating portions of the fleece to make life easy and minimize waste. Use your hands and fingertips to tell where the quality changes; when you detect a change, separate the portion off.

- Remove any dirty, stained or otherwise unusable wool from around the edges.
- Locate the center back of the fleece and set aside any mushy or unsound wool caused by weathering.
- Separate the rump wool, which will be similar in character to the back wool but coarse and more sound because it is less weathered.
- Separate the britch (the outside of the hind leg), which will provide the coarsest (strongest) wool in the fleece. If the sheep has a tendency to produce kemp fibres (short, coarse fibers that are chalky in appearance if white but may also be

Sorting a fleece.

	Most desirable
	Good
	Least desirable

colored), they may show up in this area.
- For garment making, the shoulder wool is usually the most desirable portion; the upper sides will be the next best.

Every section of the fleece can be used but probably not in the same garment. The strong, sometimes hairy britch pieces can be used for rugs or upholstery, or for stuffing toys or cushions. There are many uses for oddments.

WOOL FAULTS

On the whole, fleeces with noticeable faults should be avoided. Occasionally however, you may discover a previously unnoticed problem or have consciously decided to accept a minor fault because the fleece has other virtues. For these occasions,

173

	Symptoms	Fault	Cause	Emergency First Aid
STAINS	Diffuse yellow stain that won't wash out. The most commonly seen yellow stain	Canary stain	Complex combination of weather and fleece characteristics	Dye the fleece before using and/or drum-card to blend the stained fleece evenly
	Deep buttery yellow-colored yolk on the greasy fleece	Scourable yellow	High-quality feed and a genetic tendency to produce a yellow yolk	Not really a fault because this can be washed out completely. However, make certain it does not mask other unscourable stains
	Yellow stain in a distinct horizontal band across the staple associated with the presence of hard brittle material. Usually in black wool	Yellow banding or fleece rot	Continued wetness of the sheep's skin causing inflammation	Can be removed with careful and thorough washing but may be associated with unscourable canary stain
	Green and/or brown stain, purple stain, red-yellow or apricot stain, blue stain, either diffuse or in horizontal bands	Bacterial stains	Active bacterial colonies in the fleece	Remove affected parts of the fleece or overdye
	Black tar-like tips on the staples	Black fungus tip	Fungal infection	Remove affected tips before preparation
	Black stain on staple beginning at the tips and extending towards the butt end.	Charcoal stain	Stains caused by brushing against recently burned vegetation	Thorough washing to clean as much stain as possible. Remove any remaining stained tips before preparation
	Light pink to red color on the staple tips	Pink tip	Photo-chemical reaction in wet fleeces	Wash thoroughly. Remove any remaining stained tips before preparation
	Brightly colored waxy stains on portions of the fleece	Brands and markers	Use of unscourable markers by the grower	Remove the affected fleece *before* washing to prevent staining of clean wool
FOREIGN MATTER	Straw, seeds, and grass embedded in the wool	Vegetable contamination	Dirty or weedy pastures. Feeding practices	Remove large burr heads before washing. Combing or drum-carding may remove more contaminants than other preparation methods
	Granular material in the fleece and/or larger dark pupal cases cemented to the wool fibers with red/brown discoloration	Insect damage	Insect excreta and pupal cases left in the fleece	Unless the infestation is bad, there should be no damage to the fleece. Remove badly affected portions and wash remainder thoroughly
	Long vertical "strings" of yolky material in the staple	Stringy yolk	Increased yolk production by isolated patches of skin	Avoid fleeces with heavy contamination. Thorough washing will remove the stringy material
	Wool fibers cemented together into small, hardened bundles	Mycotic dermatitis	Skin infection	Fiber usually undamaged. Careful washing will remove hardened "cement"

	Symptoms	Fault	Cause	Emergency First Aid
STRUCTURE	Wool breaks at the same place in the staple during preparation. Thinning of the staple that can often be seen by holding it up to the light	Break	Illness, trauma, or poor feeding that interferes with wool growth	If at either end of staple, pull off and discard smallest portion. Drum-card to blend short and long fibers.
	Excessive waste and broken fibers during preparation. No discernible pattern in the position of breakage	Tenderness	Nutritional deficiency or seasonal changes in wool growth	Flick-card to determine if waste is acceptable, then flick-card or pre-prepare with care and drum- or hand-card to blend short and long fibers
	Staples are difficult to pull apart and there is the sound of breaking fibers when they are separated	Cotting or matting	Interaction of fleece characteristics, moisture, and feed	Time consuming to process and will seriously diminish yarn quality. Remove badly affected portions of the fleece. Pick or tease then card to blend broken and whole fibers
	Clumps of short fibers at the butt end of the staples	Second shear	Overlapping cuts during shearing cut off the end of the staple	Remove the second cuts before preparation
	Fibers rotted and fused together into a pink-colored indistinct mass. Damage usually localized in the staple and the fleece.	Pink rot	Bacterial infection	Remove and discard the affected portions of the fleece
	Tapered staple with long, dry, and brittle tips	Weathering	The action of sunlight and weather on wool, particularly prevalent on the back	Remove the brittle portion of the staple before preparation
	Inconsistent crimp and fiber diameter or irregular crimp, poor style	Doggy wool	Usually found in portions of fleeces from older sheep	Remove affected portions and discard or blend with normal portions of the fleece

consult the table on the preceding pages summarizing the major wool faults, their symptoms, causes, and suggestions to minimize the effect of the fault on spinning and on the finished yarn. Be aware that minimizing a fault is not a remedy. The old saying about the silk purse and sow's ear still holds true!

One problem that can rear its ugly head at a later date is that of *yellow stain*, often called *canary stain*. On purchase, the fleece may have looked fine, but lurking inside was a disposition to yellowing, usually because of an alkalinity-acidity imbalance in the suint, or sweat, trapped in the fiber. Under certain storage conditions, such as when fleece is packed in a plastic bag and stored where temperature changes occur, yellowing can take place. There are several other reasons, some listed below, not to use plastic bags for general storage.

STORING FLEECE

There is nothing as wonderful to spin as a freshly shorn fleece straight from the animal's back. Few of us have the opportunity to experience this joy, and so we have to plan ahead to ensure having a range of wool always on hand to provide suitable material for our needs: something fine, something in the long-wool range, some down type, and perhaps a specialty fleece. Most spinners seem to collect fleeces like postage stamps. If only they took up as little room! No matter how much is stored at home, the sight and feel of a delicious fleece creates temptation of such magnitude that only strong discipline can contain it.

Wool that has been shorn for some time, even a period of years, will retain its original quality unless it has been affected by storage conditions. Time itself will not diminish the quality of the product (unlike its effect on meat, fruit, or vegetables), but other factors could cause disappointment.

Plastic bags are suitable for wool storage only when the wool is kept at a constant temperature. If you put some wool into a plastic bag and set it in the sun for a few minutes, you will quickly notice condensation forming on the inside of the bag. The combination of temperature changes and moisture may damage the fleece or bring out its tendency to stain.

Heavy paper bags or cardboard cartons are much preferred to plastic bags. Unbleached muslin is an ideal storage material. It breathes with the fiber and allows moisture to escape. Old pillowcases make good storage bags, too, and you don't have to make the bags! If possible then, store your fleece in cloth bags and label each bag with a tag with the type of wool, when and where it was obtained, and any comments you wish to add. Tie the bag tightly at the top.

Moth larvae can be very destructive if given the freedom of the wool room. Paper bags, newsprint, cloth, and plastic do not deter the little pests. In one extreme case, a previously full bag of wool was reduced to a crumpled sack on the floor! The entire contents had been devoured; it is fair to report that the aroma was not pleasant. So do protect your treasure from this unpleasant end just as you would when storing winter clothing.

Washing wool before storing may help protect and preserve your wool and make it more pleasant to use when the time comes. Moths are less attracted to clean wool than they are to greasy fleece, although washing is no guarantee that they will stay away. Long-stored greasy wool will very likely need to be washed before it can be used because cold weather causes the grease to solidify, making the fleece hard to work. Washing the fleece can turn a disaster into a success story, but because washing fresh fleece is more pleasant, and usually easier than washing one which has been stored for any length of time, why not wash the wool before you pack it away?

WASH BEFORE YOU SPIN?

Which is better: spinning in the grease, or spinning clean fiber? Different spinners hold differing points of view. Particularly when working with fine wool, it is very difficult to remove the wool wax, or grease, after the wool has been spun, even more so if the yarn being spun is fine. The extra twist needed for fine yarn holds the wax inside the yarn. Washing will remove the wax on the surface, and initially the yarn will feel clean, but soon the grease held in the yarn's core will begin to work its way to the surface and the yarn or garment will feel waxy again. Rewashing removes only the surface wax and the cycle starts again. This can go on for ages!

The same is true of dirt: once spun in, it is not easy to get out, and instead of a beautiful white or clearly colored garment, you may have one with dull grayish overtones.

Washing a natural-colored fleece may provide a surprise or two. Colored fleeces may harbor more dirt than white fleeces although this is not obvious. After washing, a colored fleece can be quite a different color from its former one! You will know exactly what you are working with if you wash before you spin. In stronger, more lustrous fleeces, the grease in the spun yarn is less of a problem, but several other advantages to washing them still apply.

- Your much loved and expensive spinning wheel will keep its original condition much longer if you spin washed wool.
- The orifice will not become clogged with grease.
- Your carpets and clothing will not have to harbor the pile of dirt that inevitably accompanies the spinning of wool in the grease.
- No longer will the family complain about "that dreadful smell" and you may find that the pleasure and ease of handspinning are greater than you imagined.

If you are concerned about the loss of moisture protection for an outer garment, wash the wool with only warm water and a minimum of detergent. This will leave some grease in the wool while removing the dirt and unpleasant odor. (Washing methods are described on pages 210–213.) Grease left in the garment will, however, attract and hold dirt and dust more quickly than a garment made from well-washed yarn.

INSECT DAMAGE

Two main kinds of insect pests damage wool products: clothes moths and carpet beetles. In each case, it is the larvae which are destructive. The female clothes moth lays her eggs (up to 200 at a time) which hatch in about 3 to 21 days. The larvae move about very little, no more than a few inches. The female carpet beetle lays her eggs (30 to 100 at a time) in a dark dusty corner. When they hatch (in about 6 to 20 days) they go out and seek a suitable food source.

For woolen sweaters and similar garments, the most effective method of preventing insect damage is light and cleanliness. Never leave a soiled sweater lying in a dark drawer, chest, or corner. Soiled areas provide extra nourishment and presumably, flavor to the meal. Keratin, the protein found in wool and other hair fibers, is the preferred food of clothes moth larvae; carpet beetle larvae include many other protein sources, including silk, in their diet. A larva can sever a fine wool fiber with one snap of its jaws, so fine wool is a favorite. A coarser fiber may take a little more effort, but these little pests have real staying power.

Articles of wool that are stored or hung in the same place for long periods of time, such as wall hangings, will benefit from periodic airing and dusting. They can also be sprayed on the back with an insecticide repeated according to the effective life of the spray used. Mothballs release a toxic vapor which is effective only in enclosed spaces such as drawers and cupboards. When storing bags of fleece, include a few mothballs or flakes of naphthalene wrapped in a piece of gauze, and tightly close the neck of the bag.

Naphthalene and paradichlorobenzene are fumigants, not repellents. Years ago, our grandmothers used camphor chests to store blankets and winter clothing. Camphor is an effective fumigant and repellent, as is a long-lasting synthetic camphor produced from pine turpentine. Both are available today.

CAVEAT

One final word of advice. We have all known spinners (these two included) who have been asked to spin some yarn for a farmer friend who has said that she or he would love to knit a sweater from the wool of her or his flock. A good farmer is not necessarily good at selecting wool, and you may find yourself with a totally unsuitable fleece. It is time to do one of two things, both challenging for the spinner. Both involve facing the donor with the cold hard facts and perhaps raising his or her appreciation for the wool that has been taken for granted on the farm.

The first possibility, if the fleece is suitable for *some* purpose, is to redirect the farmer's vision toward an appropriate project: say, an entry rug rather than a sweater.

The second possibility, if the fleece is beyond reasonable limits of pleasant spinning, is to suggest that you sell the fleece and with the proceeds buy some wool that will fit the need. Samples of your work may persuade the farmer that handspun yarn can be of such quality that this will be the best route to take. And who knows—the farmer may be persuaded to alter some husbandry techniques to produce better wool, and you may acquire a fine and acceptable fleece from the farm in a subsequent year. The farmer may even end up with a secondary income selling fine fleeces to handspinners.

Whatever course you choose, do not struggle in an attempt to make something wonderful from a trashy or unsound fleece. The same advice holds good for new spinners. Don't be misled into thinking that anything goes to practice on. How many times have we seen an experienced spinner give some scraps of fleece to a beginner "to practice on". The beginner needs the best fleece available. There are plenty of other struggles getting that wheel to obey commands without having the misery of scrappy fleece to contend with as well.

Treat your skills with respect and use the very best, most suitable fleece you are able to procure.

8
BLENDING WOOL

Blended fibers create a yarn which combines the properties of all of its components. There are two major reasons for blending wool with other fibers: to create a yarn with properties not available from a single fiber alone or to stretch a rare or expensive fiber and make it go further. Sometimes a blend is made for both reasons.

In general, when you select fibers for blending, each should add to or support the other's strong points. Just what the strong points of a given fiber are will depend on the final use you have in mind for the yarn.

For instance, if you choose silk for its softness and luster, blending it with Cheviot (which has almost no luster and a crisp hand) doesn't make sense. Blending silk with Polwarth, however, will add loft and elasticity without sacrificing softness, and will preserve much of the luster.

Matching wool with another fiber for blending requires considering the independent properties of both and the job that you want the yarn to do. Aim to match the properties that you wish to preserve or enhance, and to supply any characteristics you wish to add.

Hard-wearing knitted fabric, suitable for outerwear. Two-ply spun from Suffolk and Romney blended together on a drum carder.

Three-ply yarn spun from Clun Forest blended with an equal weight of kid mohair.
The Clun Forest adds loft and elasticity to the softness and sheen of the mohair.

PROPORTIONS

The "correct" proportion of wool to another fiber depends entirely on the look, feel, and other characteristics that you want to achieve in the yarn. Although it can be useful for future work to know what proportions you have used in a blend, accurate measurement is not essential to producing the effect you want. You can compose blends at random if that suits you. The benefit of measuring is that you can reproduce your results another time.

Weight is the most consistent and accurate way to measure fibers for a blend, but by no means the only one. If you are blending fiber that has already been prepared into top or sliver, you can use measured lengths. In a pinch, even standard handfuls of loose fiber will do. The smaller the quantity that you are able to process at one time, the more important it is to measure accurately if you want a homogeneous blend with a minimum of bother.

Fibers for a blend should be weighed or measured into standard units. These units may but do not have to correspond to the amount of fiber in each finished batt or sliver. They should be small enough so that, if necessary, you can further subdivide the fiber into quantities that are convenient to process at one time. For instance, to prepare a blend that is 75 percent wool and 25 percent silk, you might weigh out the wool in 3/4-ounce lots and silk in 1/4-ounce lots. If the hand cards you want to use will only hold 1/8 ounce at a time, divide the lots of wool and silk into eight pieces of equal size, and match each piece of wool to one of silk.

Blending fibers of different lengths on wool combs often results in an uneven distribution of the fibers in the top.

COMBINING THE RIGHT FLEECE WITH THE RIGHT FIBER

Fiber length. Although it's not strictly necessary to match the lengths of the fibers to be blended, doing so simplifies preparation and spinning. With fibers of equivalent length, any of the preparation methods that permit blending will give you a homogeneous yarn. When one type of fiber is longer than the other, the preparation method must be chosen with more care.

Hand-carding and drum-carding are usually the better methods when the lengths vary, or you may choose to have a custom carding service prepare the blend for you. If you choose commercial carding, check beforehand that the carder has equipment that can handle your fibers.

Combing is usually a poor choice for blending fibers of uneven length. The goal of combing is to separate short and tangled fibers from long fibers. If you attempt to comb a blend of fibers, you may find your long fibers in the top and your short fibers stuck in the combs. In addition, your longest fibers will be in the first section of top, and the shorter fibers will be drawn off last.

A hand-carded rolag does a good job of keeping uneven fibers well mixed. Because you'll be drafting from all parts of the fibers and not just the ends, long and short fibers will feed equally into the yarn.

If you want your fibers in a more parallel arrangement or need to prepare large quantities of a blend, drum-carding produces a very homogeneous mix. You can make drum-carded batts that are especially smooth if you flick-card or comb the wool before blending it.

When there is a significant difference between fiber lengths (for example, wool and cotton), treat the finished batts with care in order to preserve the blend. Instead of pulling wide strips of batt into sliver, tear each batt into very narrow strips that are ready for spinning without further work. It is the pulling that may cause the long and short fibers to separate.

Drafting will also require a light hand. The long fibers tend to draft out first, leaving clumps of shorter fibers behind or as chunks in the yarn. The beginning and end of each length of sliver are potential trouble spots, because the long fibers usually protrude from the ends. Join onto the next length before getting to the absolute end of the one you're working from.

If the fibers you wish to blend are not the same length, you can adjust them. You can shorten the length by simply cutting wool staples in half or by trimming either the butt or the tip ends: bend it to fit, paint it to match. Because the tips are the less desirable portion of the staple (having been subjected to the most wear and tear already), it's usually best to snip from this end. Be aware that trimming may influence the overall color of a natural-colored or dyed fleece, because in many cases the tips are a different color from that of the rest of the staple.

Elasticity and loft. Two of the most important and closely related properties that wool can lend to other fibers are elasticity and loft. The amount of elasticity in a fleece is related to the type of crimp it has.

With their well-developed spiral crimp, down-type fleeces have the most elasticity. Fine wools are a close second and divide roughly into two groups for crimp pattern: Rambouillet and breeds with Rambouillet blood, which have well-developed, irregular, three-dimensional crimp; and Merino and breeds with Merino blood, with well-developed, well organized crimp. Fine crossbred wools or longwools, which have a crimp pattern similar to that of Merino but with fewer crimps per inch, also have a good to moderate amount of elasticity. Longwools and strong crossbred fleeces, with their long wavy or curly crimp, have the least.

When selecting a fleece which will contribute elasticity and loft to a blend, consider also the softness required to match the other fiber and the durability needed in the yarn. For loft and softness, one of the fine wools would be excellent. To preserve as much luster as possible, a Merino or part Merino breed (such as Polwarth, any comeback type, or fine New Zealand Halfbred) would be a good choice. Where softness is not essential but resilience and bulk are important, one of the down-type fleeces deserves consideration. Crossbred fleeces offer moderate elasticity and good wearing properties for combining with stronger fibers, whereas longwools and strong crossbreds are best left for projects requiring a very hard-wearing, coarse blend with little elasticity and loft.

Softness. How soft a fleece feels is almost directly related to the fineness of the wool fiber. The higher the count (or the smaller the micron measurement), the softer the fleece. Conversely, the lower the count (the higher the micron measurement), the harsher the handle. Although a considerable range of fiber diameters can be found within each of the three broad groups of fleeces (fine wools, longwools, and down-types), if softness is a priority, look for a suitable fleece among the fine wools. Most down-type fleeces fall in the medium range, whereas crossbred and long-wool fleeces range from medium to strong.

Durability. Wear resistance comes from a combination of resilience and fiber diameter. Longwool and crossbred fleeces are usually very hard-wearing. Down-type wools, strong fine wools, and fine crossbred fleeces are good for moderate wear, whereas the remaining fine fleeces are better known for softness than ruggedness.

Washing, finishing, and fabric care. The care requirements of the fibers that you choose to blend together must be compatible within the context of the yarn's use. If the piece that you are planning will require frequent washing, there must be a washing method that will clean both fibers effectively and yet preserve their desired qualities.

Most fibers will shrink and/or take up to some extent when washed, and this can change the characteristics of the yarn considerably, particularly in a blend. Felting shrinkage occurs when heat, moisture, and movement cause the fibres to move (see DFE page 17), becoming entangled and shortening the length of the yarn. Take-up or relaxation shrinkage occurs when fibers have been extended during a process, such as spinning, but on exposure to moisture return to their original length. Wool shrinks and takes up more than most other fibers, and a differential in shrinkage can have quite a profound effect on the yarn. This isn't necessarily a drawback—in fact, it can be used very effectively as a design tool.

Thus, it's a good idea to wash any finished yarn before using it so that you can take into account any changes in diameter, elasticity, color, or texture. This will guard against nasty surprises in the finished piece, such as having a perfectly fitting sweater suddenly become two sizes too small after the first wash or a perfectly smooth yarn become knobbly and textured.

Dry cleaning carries the least risk of unanticipated shrinkage or change in a fabric and may be suitable treatment for an uncertain blend if the piece cannot be washed easily or doesn't need frequent cleaning.

The components of a blend can affect the results of dyeing as well. Different fibers frequently take up dye in different ways, and fibers may behave differently when in the dyepot together than when dyed alone. If you intend to use color in a blended yarn, ascertain ahead of time which type of dye works with all your components and whether it is better to dye before or after blending and spinning.

Dye information sheets will state for which fibers the dyeing method is suitable, and at what temperature each will absorb the dye. If your fibers are very different, the fiber that absorbs at a lower temperature may consume the bulk of the dye, leaving the other fiber considerably lighter. Union dyes can dye several different fibers with the same dyebath, but each fiber may be a slightly different shade. These differences in color can be used much like the difference in shrinkage and take up between fibers. Instead of producing problems, subtle color differences can result in yarns that have more depth and life than a single-fiber yarn.

BLENDING WITH WOOL COMBS

If the fiber lengths are comparable, a preparation blended on combs will produce the smoothest possible yarn. However, this method results in a considerable amount of waste, both of the wool and of the fiber blended with it.

If the fibers you are blending have not already been prepared for spinning, you can load them onto the combs and prepare and blend at the same time. For a blend of mohair and wool, for example, lash on one row of wool followed by a row of mohair. Continue to alternate rows of wool and mohair until the comb is loaded. Another option is to load the combs with fiber arranged as a checkerboard, with mohair and wool alternating across each row.

When the comb is loaded, comb as usual (see pages 196–198). It sometimes takes more passes to blend the fibers than it would to prepare each kind separately.

If the fiber to be blended with wool is already prepared for spinning (for example, silk in top or sliver form), you may be able to reduce waste by combing the wool separately first. After you have combed it and drawn it off into a top, weigh out appropriate units of wool top and silk sliver and reload the combs. Load the fiber in alternating rows or a checkerboard, using staple-length pieces of each fiber. Once again, follow the general method for combing until the blend is satisfactory. Draw off the blended top.

BLENDING WITH A DRUM CARDER

A drum carder is a wonderful tool for blending. It gives a consistent blend whether or not you have the equipment for accurate measuring, and it is ideal when you want to process a large quantity of fiber. Measure out the fibers to be blended in the proportion you want in the final blend. Follow the general directions for drum carding (see pages 192–194), feeding the fibers onto the carder in about the correct proportions.

Wool usually feeds easily onto the drum although some noncrimped or short fibers may be troublesome. After they are on the drum for the first time and blended with the wool, however, there is usually no further problem. Putting a fine layer of wool on the drum first will usually make it easier to take the batt off when it's finished.

The easiest and fastest method of getting the fibers onto the carder initially is to alternate sections of each fiber, spreading them across the width of the feed tray before feeding in. Just as in single-fiber drum carding, put all the fiber through the carder once, then split, shuffle, and recard until the blend is satisfactory.

The number of times you split and recard the batt will depend on how even you want the blend to be. A truly homogeneous blend will require more passes through the machine than does a simple preparation.

Hint: If the fibers drift over the surface of the main drum or collect on the infeed roller, try the following trick. Spread out a thin layer of the blending fiber and then spread out the wool in a thin layer to cover. Feed both fibers on together. *Another hint:* If this is still unsuccessful, you can bypass the infeed roller by placing the blending fiber directly onto the main drum. With the main drum stationary, catch small quantities of the fiber on the teeth and pat them into place with your hand. Rotate the drum a few inches and repeat to distribute the fiber as evenly as possible.

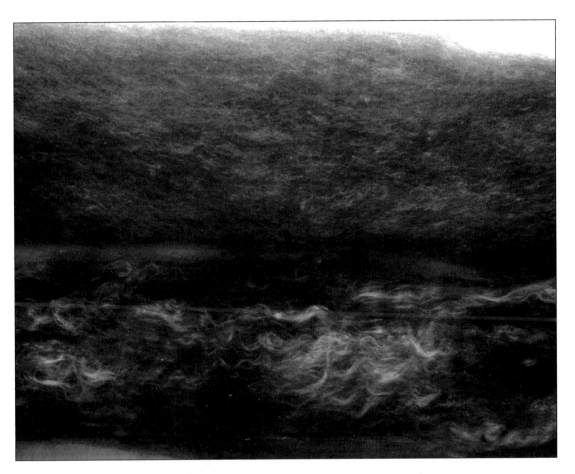

Brown Cormo and Bombyx mori *silk. Bottom: First pass through the drum carder. Top: Fourth pass through the drum carder.*

BLENDING WITH HAND CARDERS

Hand carders are very effective blending tools, the only drawback being the small quantity which can be processed at a time. For a measured blend, weigh as small a quantity of fiber as your scales will allow. If that is still too large (and it probably will be), divide it by eye into single carder loads.

To load the cards, place a fine layer of wool on one card. Follow this with the blending fiber and end with another fine layer of wool. For a 50/50 blend of wool and silk, the first layer of wool should comprise one-fourth of the total amount of fiber that you put on the card, the silk, one-half, and the final layer of wool the remaining one-quarter. Now proceed according to the general carding instructions (see pages 190–192). Because the object is to blend the fibers as well as to prepare them, you may need to take more passes with the cards

Three-ply yarn of flick-carded Targheee blended with pima cotton on a fine drum carder. The yarn has the feel of cotton but the elasticity of wool.

than would be required for preparation alone.

For a more even blend, take the finished batts from the cards without rolling them. When all the fiber has been used up, split each finished batt in two and lightly recard each half with half of another batt. When you're satisfied with the blend, roll the batts into rolags.

When working with more than one fiber, there is an almost overwhelming temptation to overload the cards. Many carding problems can be quickly solved simply by loading less fiber on the cards.

Hint: Carding will be most efficient if all fibers are prepared first. Flick-card, comb, or tease any unprepared fleece or blending fiber to make carding go faster and more smoothly.

BLENDING DIFFERENT TYPES OF WOOL

Handspinners have on the whole been reluctant to take advantage of the flexibility offered by blending different types of fleeces together, and yet the wool industry has made extensive use of this process for years. By blending wools with different properties, you can improve the performance and manage the characteristics of a particular fleece or yarn. You can stretch bits and pieces of good leftover fleece into whole garments by combining them with similar or different types of fleece, without sacrificing quality or utility. Fleece of a single color can be extended into a range of tints and shades if it is mixed with white or with other colored fleece.

The guidelines above for blending wool with other fibers apply equally well to all-wool blends. In fact, you will probably find that they are easier to handle than blends with other fibers. For instance, differences in staple length are usually more manageable in all-wool blends.

When selecting fleeces to combine, always keep the final use in mind, aiming to match the properties that you wish to preserve or enhance and to supply any characteristics that you wish to add. Factors to consider when matching fleeces and purpose are softness, elasticity, loft, durability, and finishing.

TERMS AND TECHNIQUES

METHODS OF FIBER PREPARATION

The preparation of fiber plays a major role in the quality or type of yarn that will be produced.

FLICK-CARDING

Flick-carding opens up individual locks of wool for spinning without removing the shorter fibers. The flick carder, sometimes called a flicker, has a flat, rectangular head, covered on one surface with carding cloth, and a handle attached to the back of the head. It is the flicking motion that distinguishes it from combing, where the tool is drawn through the locks. Lay a small piece of leather, vinyl, or canvas on your lap to protect your skin and clothing from the carder. You will use this as a base for your work.

Grasp the butt end of a lock firmly in one hand. Holding the flick carder in the other hand, near the end of the handle farthest from the head, flick the tips of the staple. The motion consists of bringing the carder down onto the staple until the teeth are engaged in the fiber, then quickly pulling the carder up and away from the staple; the carding surface should lie parallel to the fibers. The carder appears to bounce off the staple, rather than draw through it. Three or four fast flicks in quick succession should open out the tip half of

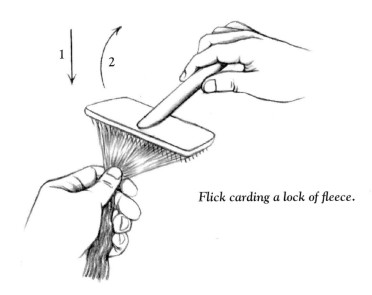

Flick carding a lock of fleece.

the staple into a fan of fiber. Now grasp the tip end of the staple firmly and repeat the process, opening the butt end.

The fibers in the flicked locks should remain neatly aligned but will now be separate from each other. Hold the locks up to the light to make sure there are no streaks of shadow made by fibers still clumped together.

Flick-carding can be used as a preparation method in itself, and it is also useful as a preliminary to other preparation methods, such as drum-carding and blending (whether with hand carders, drum carder, or wool combs). Flicked locks can increase the speed or smoothness of the subsequent preparation.

HAND-CARDING

Hand-carding is a traditional means of preparing fleece, particularly for the spinning of woolen yarn. Hand carders (sometimes called double carders) are expensive tools; they should be kept clean and their teeth protected from damage.

The carding cloth, usually a sheet of rubberized canvas or leather into which wire teeth are anchored, on a pair of carders will dictate the type of fleece which can best be prepared with them. The finer the wire of the teeth and the closer their spacing, the finer the fleece or fiber that you will be able to card satisfactorily. Coarse carders, often called "wool" carders, are usually used for wool. "Cotton" carders have fine carding cloth and can be used for other fine fibers, such as fine wool, silk, angora, and cashmere.

Ideally, the fiber to be carded should be about as long as the length of the carder from toe to heel.

There are two schools of thought regarding the need to use a given carder only in the right hand and the other only in the left. Some people find that carders that have been used constantly in the same hands work more smoothly than carders that have not. Others think it doesn't matter. The choice is yours. For ease of description, we'll refer to "right" and "left" carders. The *heel* of the carder is the long edge to which the handle is attached; its *toe* is the opposite long edge.

1. Place the left carder on your lap and, starting at one side, attach the butt end of a staple of fleece along the carder's heel, about 1/2 inch (1 cm) from the edge. Lightly attach the remainder of the staple to the carder. Continue laying staples onto the carder in this way until the surface of the carding cloth is covered. It is always better to underload, rather than overload, a carder. The loading process is called *charging* the carder.

2. Pick up both carders, holding them for optimum comfort as follows: When the teeth are facing *up*, your palm should be facing up. When the teeth are facing *down*, your palm should be facing down. Holding the right carder with its teeth facing down, begin brushing it across the left carder. Start at the fringe of wool protruding from the toe of the left carder and work your way up toward the heel with each successive brushing movement. Brush two or three times, making sure that the fringe of fiber at the toe of the left carder does not get caught up and looped back onto the teeth. The teeth of the two carders should not engage but should be gently drawn across the fiber. Some of the fiber will now have been transferred to the right carder.

3. You now need to transfer the remaining fleece from the left carder to the

Hand-Carding

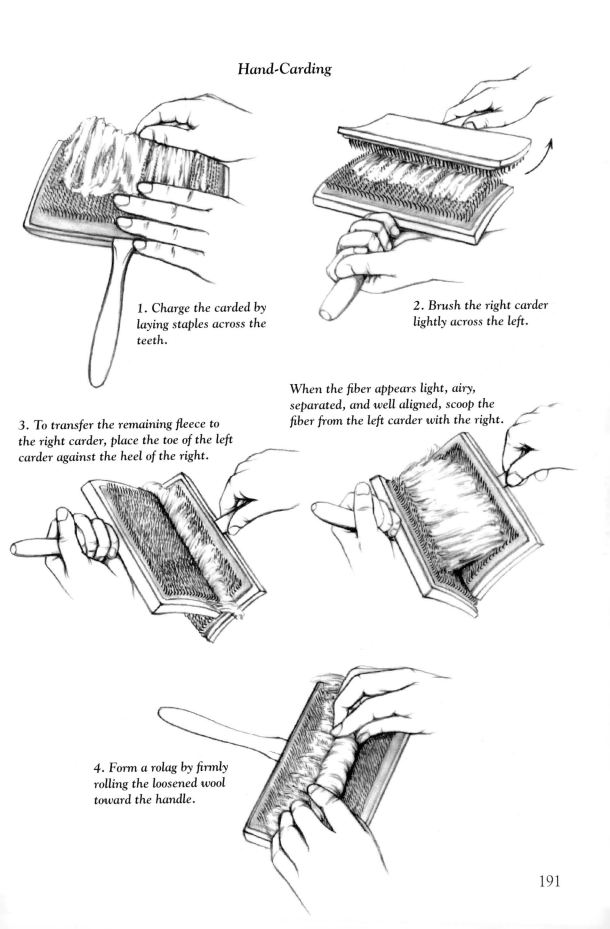

1. Charge the carded by laying staples across the teeth.

2. Brush the right carder lightly across the left.

3. To transfer the remaining fleece to the right carder, place the toe of the left carder against the heel of the right.

When the fiber appears light, airy, separated, and well aligned, scoop the fiber from the left carder with the right.

4. Form a rolag by firmly rolling the loosened wool toward the handle.

right carder. Turn both carders face up and touch the toe of the left carder to the heel of the right carder, then gently lift the right carder, keeping the toe edge close to the surface of the left carder and scooping the fiber from the left.

The right carder should now hold almost all the fiber. With the right carder teeth up and the left carder face down, brush the fiber on the right carder with the left carder two or three times, again starting at the toe and working toward the heel, still keeping the fringe straight. The fiber should appear light, airy, separated, and well aligned. If it doesn't, transfer the fleece back onto the left carder. With both carders teeth up, touch the toe of the right carder to the heel of the left. Gently lift the left carder, scooping the fiber from the right. Now brush with the right carder again.

4. When the fiber is well brushed, transfer it (using the heel-to-toe method) from carder to carder twice. This should leave it lying lightly on the top of one of the carders. To form it into a rolag, place the carder containing the fleece on your lap and, starting from the toe end, firmly roll the fleece toward the handle and off the carder. The fleece should now look like a thin, elegant sausage.

If you plan to use the carded fiber as a worsted-type preparation, keep the fibers parallel by rolling them off the carder from side to side, instead of from heel to toe.

Apart from the traditional use of carders for the preparation of rolags, they are great for blending fibers and for aligning fibers that have become untidy through some other process such as dyeing. Blending is dealt with in more depth on pages 185–187.

DRUM-CARDING

The first step to effective use of a drum carder is keeping the machine in good working order. Follow the manufacturer's directions for lubrication with regard both to the type of lubricant and the frequency of application. Keep the bearings free of stray fiber and clean the drums carefully and thoroughly between jobs.

If your machine permits, adjust the drums so that the teeth of the main drum are as close as possible to the infeed roller (also called the *licker-in*) without actually making contact. You can usually do this by moving the drums gradually closer until you hear the teeth just meshing as the handle turns. Back the drums off a fraction until they are no longer touching. Place a piece of white paper under the drums to help you see the gap between them more clearly, or adjust the drums so that you can slip a piece of thin paper between them.

Consider carefully the advantages of using only washed fleece on your drum carder: it cards more smoothly and is easier on the machine and the fiber. Unwashed fleece leaves a sticky deposit of wool grease on the teeth and drums of the carder. This grease collects dirt and, if not cleaned off regularly, will contaminate clean fiber. Greasy fleece also tends to tangle more than clean fleece, which leads to the stretching and breaking of fibers. For this reason, an unwashed fleece usually requires a coarser carding cloth than the same fleece would if washed. If you wish to prepare both greasy and washed fleeces, consider reserving a separate drum or even a separate machine for each.

Spending some time in preparing the fleece for carding pays off two ways: you will spend less time at the carder, and your

Drum-Carding

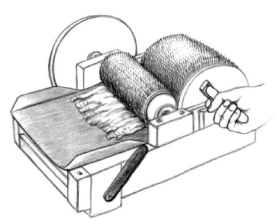

Feed the prepared locks under the in-feed roller.

Use a doffing rod to make a separation in the batt.

Pull the batt off toward the rear of the main drum.

spinning will be faster and more pleasant. With your fingers, spread out the tips and cut ends of the locks of fleece, working out any lumps or tangles. Remove second cuts and any hay or seeds.

1. Gradually feed the locks under the in-feed roller. If the locks are "snatched" onto the drum, allow the weight of your hand to rest on them as they move under the infeed roller. How much weight to place on the locks will depend on your machine. With too much pressure, the locks may wrap themselves around the infeed roller; with too little, the locks will tangle as they go onto the main drum.

2. As you feed in subsequent locks, distribute the fiber evenly across the width of the drum. Continue until the drum is full. You'll know it's full when fiber starts to drift over the surface of the main drum or to collect on the infeed roller.

3. Use a doffing rod to make a separation in the batt, working section by section across the open strip on the main drum. Remove the batt from the drum by turning the crank backward and gently pulling the fiber free of the teeth. Put the batts aside so that they can be easily separated later.

Continue carding until all the fiber has been processed once.

4. Separate each batt into several equal lengthwise strips (four is usually a good number) and combine strips from several different batts for the second carding. For every group of four newly combined strips, spread each strip widthwise until it is equal to the width of the infeed roller and feed it onto the carder, again using the weight of your hand to gently retard the fiber and prevent snatching. Continue to process all the groups of four strips.

Repeat this separating-and-recombining step as many times as necessary to achieve the desired result. The finished batts should be uniform and fluffy with no streaks or clumps of uncarded fiber. For most clean fleeces, three or four times through the carder is sufficient.

Hint: If you find an unacceptable number of tiny dense clumps of fibers (called *neps*) in your batts, extract a few and examine them carefully. With a needle, tease the neps apart to see whether they are made up of short or long fibers. Short-fiber neps are probably the result of second cuts or of brittle tips which have broken off; you can reduce their numbers by removing the tips and any other short fibers from the staples before feeding them onto the drum. Long-fiber neps are made up of normal-length fibers that have wound themselves up into a ball. You can usually minimize them by using a finer carding cloth.

One word of caution. Although drum carders are sometimes used as the tool of last resort to prepare a fleece that has serious faults, you will never get out anything better than went in. The only way to achieve the best possible results from a poor fleece is by spending some time and thought figuring out how to work around or minimize the fleece's drawbacks. Putting the wool through a drum carder may be the answer—if you take the time to prepare it properly; then again, it may not.

PICKING OR TEASING

Picking or teasing means simply opening and separating the fibers of the wool staples, to make them ready for immediate spinning or, more usually, for either hand- or drum-carding. Picking can be done by hand or with a hand-operated mechanical picker. Either washed or greasy fleece can be picked, but, as with carding, washed fleece will usually require less effort, and more vegetable matter can be removed during processing from a clean fleece.

To tease by hand, carefully pull out individual staples and spread the fibers open to separate them. Pay particular attention to the tip and butt ends. A teased staple should be a fluffy mass of loose fibers.

Teasing by hand.

A mechanical picker is more efficient for processing large quantities of fleece or for tackling large blending jobs. As with other equipment, your picker should be clean, properly maintained, and in good working order. Follow the manufacturer's directions for care, lubrication, and safety precautions. Pickers which are not in use should be carefully secured to prevent accidents. You may want to wear leather gloves and a sturdy leather apron to protect yourself from accidental contact with the cradle teeth.

Adjust the cradle to leave at least 1/8 inch (3mm) clearance between the upper and lower points. If the width of your picking bench or table allows it, place a box be-hind and below the picker to collect the picked fiber that drops out with every swing.

Feed fleece in from the front, taking care not to let the cradle pick up too much fiber on each swing. Overloading will almost certainly lead to poorly picked fiber and may cause the picker to jam. Keep the swinging motions of the cradle long, al-lowing it to clear the base on every swing. When the cradle returns toward you, it will pick up more fiber. Use a gloved hand or picker claw to limit the quantity of fiber drawn into the picker with each swing.

Mechanical picker.

HAND-COMBING USING A SINGLE COMB

This method of preparation will produce a worsted-type yarn. All the short fibers, vegetable matter, and neps (which are called noils when they have been removed from the fiber after combing) will be re-moved, and the fibers will remain parallel. This method is suitable for use with the stronger, longer, lustrous fleeces. A metal dog-grooming comb with rounded teeth about 1/8 inch (3 mm) apart is an ideal tool for this purpose. Avoid using the comb from a shearing machine as it has sharp edges which tend to tear the fiber.

Firmly grasp a small bunch of staples about 1 inch (2.5 cm) from their butt ends. Holding firmly, twist the bunch immedi-ately below the spot you are gripping, so that the fibers that were initially on the bottom of the bunch are now on the top. Without losing this twist, move your grip so that your fingers are now on top of the twist. This holds the fibers firmly in your hand during combing.

Draw the comb smoothly and firmly through the fibers two or three times, or until the bundle fans out and looks light and airy. Turn the bunch of fibers around and grip again, this time 1 inch (2.5 cm) from the tip of the staple. Twist in the same manner, then comb the butt end of the fleece. When laying down the staples after combing, keep all their butt ends facing in the same direction.

Some spinners use a flick carder as a comb, drawing the teeth through the full length of the fibers. The staples are held in the hand and rest lightly on a protective surface, such as a piece of leather or vinyl, while the flick carder is drawn through them in the same manner as a comb. You'll find that combing with a flick carder produces a slightly smoother preparation with less dirt and vegetable matter, but more waste than the same wool flick-carded.

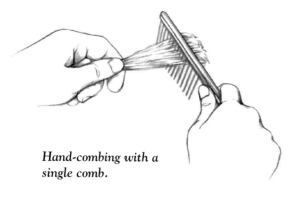

Hand-combing with a single comb.

HAND-COMBING WITH TWO COMBS

Hand-combing with two combs (also called wool-combing) removes the short and tangled fibers, leaving a smooth parallel preparation of long fibers especially suitable for worsted spinning. The advantages of a pair of wool combs over combing with a single comb are that a larger quantity of fleece can be prepared in one batch and you can blend either variations within a fleece or different fibers and fleece.

On the whole, clean, sound fleeces are preferred for wool combing because the process produces a high proportion of waste when used on a fleece with any weakness. However, combing may be the answer for some "problem" fleeces with, for example, brittle tips or too much vegetable matter. Most other preparation methods will prepare the fleece while retaining the problems, and you'll end up picking hay or neps

out of the fiber as you spin.

Although combing may waste a considerable portion of the fleece, the spinnable part will be sound and largely free from contaminants; it's a question of the value of a smaller quantity of a high-quality spinning fiber versus that of a larger quantity of a poor or mediocre preparation. Only you can make the decision based on your needs and preferences.

Of the several different types of combs, each has its peculiarities, strengths, and drawbacks. We have briefly described the basic method most often used for English combs and then noted the minor variations for using the paddle and Viking styles.

Hint: Traditionally, oil and water are used to smooth and lubricate the fleece during combing and to control static electricity. Apply the lubricant sparingly at first; you can always add more, but too much makes for a messy job. Personal preference and experience will eventually dictate your choice of lubricant, but here are a few to try. These can all be applied to the washed locks before or after loading the combs: (1) plain water, sprinkled or sprayed; (2) hair conditioner, mixed thoroughly with enough water to make a sprayable solution in a mister; (3) a few drops of olive oil and a sprinkle of water flicked on the locks by hand; (4) equal parts of olive oil and water, shaken together in a mister. If you use olive oil, plan to spin your combed wool fairly quickly. Left too long, it may become sticky.

Secure the fixed comb to its stand according to the directions that accompany your type of combs. Load locks of thoroughly washed fleece onto the fixed comb by pushing the last half-inch or so of the staple's butt end down onto the tines. When the tines are about one-quarter loaded, turn the fixed comb on its side and swing the second or moving comb downward through the locks, starting at their tips and gradually working closer to the fixed comb with each stroke. Wool will be transferred gradually from the stationary comb to the moving comb.

When all the wool has been transferred, leaving only short, tangled fibers and dirt on the fixed comb, remove the waste and repeat the process, this time transferring the fiber to the fixed comb by swinging the moving comb sideways. Continue passing the fiber from one comb to the other in this way until the mass of fiber is fluffy and uniform with no visible neps. Thread a few fibers from the combed mass through a diz (a thin disc or oval of wood, bone, horn, plastic or cardboard about 1 to 2 inches (2.5 to 5 cm) wide with a small hole in the middle through which the top is drawn from the comb) and, pushing the diz toward the comb as you go, draw the wool off the comb, hand over hand, to form a top.

Viking combs are hand-held, but the combing process is almost identical to that described above. If it is more comfortable, you may elect to exchange the fixed and moving combs when the wool has been transferred rather than reverse the combing motion; a diz is not necessary for drawing the fiber off the comb.

Paddle combs differ slightly from English and Viking combs. Fibers are combed by both the fixed and moving comb on each stroke, and when combing is complete, the combed fiber is evenly distributed between the two combs.

Drawing the combed fiber from both combs becomes important if you want to preserve the tip/butt alignment in the yarn you spin from the prepared fiber. If the tip/butt alignment is not important or if

Hand-Combing with Two Combs

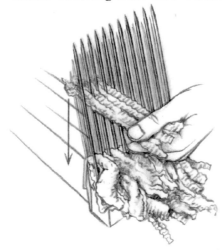

Load the fixed comb.

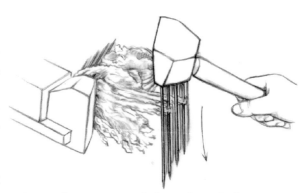

Swing the moving comb down through the locks, starting at the tips, to transfer the wool to the moving comb.

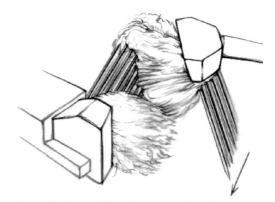

When all the wool has been transferred, swing the moving comb sideways so that the wool gradually transfers back to the stationary comb.

197

you plan to spin directly from the combs, mix the tips and butt ends of the staples while loading the combs by securing the first row of locks by their butt ends and the next row by their tips. Alternate successive rows in this manner until the fixed comb is fully loaded.

If you want to preserve the tip/butt alignment, begin as usual by loading the fixed comb and securing all staples by their butt ends. When you have finished combing, the fiber will be split between the two combs. It will be secured to one comb by its butt ends and to the other by its tips. Pull top from both combs. Wind the butt-secured top from one end and the tip-secured top from the opposite end so that the tip/butt alignments of the two match when you begin to spin.

With the fixed comb loaded and positioned with its tines up, swing the moving comb downward through the fiber, with an occasional, careful, upward swing to comb the locks at the bottom. Not all of the wool will be transferred from one comb to the other during this step, but as the moving comb becomes more fully loaded, exchange it with the fixed comb and continue.

When you're satisfied that the fibers are separate and aligned parallel, and the wool hanging in front of the tines is free from neps, distribute the fiber evenly between the combs. Draw off the top as for English combs or spin directly from the fiber held in the tines of each comb.

SLIVER, TOP, AND ROVING

These terms can be confusing. *Sliver* is a more or less continuous strand of *carded* fiber; *top* is a continuous strand of *combed*, untwisted fiber, with all the short fibers removed; and *roving* is a continuous strand of carded *or* combed fiber that has been further extended and slightly twisted.

Many people are now using commercially prepared fleece and fiber for their spinning. It is easy to be attracted by the beautiful colors that are available and by the reduction in time and effort needed for preparation. Most of these commercial preparations are either carded sliver or combed top.

It is important to know the differences between these forms because the type of

Using a Diz

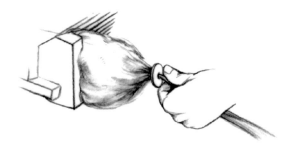

Push the diz toward the comb.

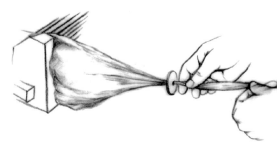

Draw off the comb hand over hand.

preparation determines whether you can spin a worsted or a woolen yarn. Just as you have to be careful about the quality of raw fleece that you purchase, so you need to be cautious when you purchase commercial preparations. Don't be seduced by magnificent colors and forget all the other desirable qualities.

Use the checklist below when purchasing prepared fiber.

- Check the handle of the wool to see if it will be suitable for your end use.
- Check the length of fiber in the sliver or top. The best-quality top will consist mostly of fibers of the same length. A sliver showing much variation in fiber length will produce a less durable yarn.
- Check the sliver or top for signs of vegetation. If the fleece is a dark natural color or dyed, you will need to take it out of the bag to check for seeds and so forth.
- Check for kemp, which will show up in dyed fleece as having missed the dye. This is poor-quality fiber. You may be able to use it, but you will have to take the kemp into account.

Some carding firms will prepare a customer's own fleece. This service gives the spinner some control over the quality of the finished product. But do not think that when you send an old, hard-to-handle fleece off to a carding company, some miracle will occur and you will get back a beautiful product. It is impossible to get anything better out than you put in! Certainly, a difficult fleece may become a little easier to handle and may look better, but in fact its quality will be exactly the same as it was before.

Garbage in, garbage out! Consider the carding service and its equipment if you're thinking of sending less than the best. Your fleece may be refused if the service is suspicious of its quality; it has its reputation and livelihood to protect. Speaking of garbage, horrendous stories are told in the industry of dangerous oddments found in fleeces, including barbed wire, tools, knitting needles, and, in one fleece which had been salted away for a year or so, the remains of a mouse nest for one unlucky carder! Is your wool beyond hope? Cut your losses and start over! When sending your fleece to a carding service, check that all the undesirable parts of the fleece such as short belly wool or soiled wool from the rear has been removed. Be sure to remove any stained sections, vegetation (particularly thistles), and fleece that is different in character from the main part (for example, hairy britch wool, matted neck wool, tender back wool, and so forth). Cotted fleece is totally unsuitable for carding. Fiber that has a break or brittle tips may snap during processing. Although fiber with breaks can be carded, brittle tips can make unpleasantly hairy fabrics as the many ends work their way out to the surface of the yarn. Weak tips can break and end up as neps or noils spread throughout the sliver. They are very difficult to remove and make for disagreeable spinning.

Fine-wool and natural-colored fleeces are particularly prone to dry tips. If the tips are weak, pull or cut them off before you send the fleece away.

Without a doubt, we prefer to wash fleece before carding it. Some carding companies offer this service as well. Some companies will process only washed fleece, and at least one that we know of reserves the right to rewash any fleece that has been sent to it for processing.

REJUVENATING SAD SLIVER, TOP, OR ROVING

Freshly carded sliver will look light and airy. After sitting under the bed or in the garage for some months (or years), it is likely to emerge looking lank and lusterless. If you spin from these compressed fibers, you will find they are difficult to draft and will make a dense, lifeless yarn. Extending puts back the air between the fibers and allows them to draft smoothly and evenly with less effort. Unwashed or poorly washed wool will need a few hours in the sun or some other warm environment to soften the grease which has set on the fiber.

To extend or predraft, break off a manageable length of sliver or top, say, 18 to 36 inches (0.5 to 1 m). (The length will vary according to your preference.) Grasp the length of fiber firmly at one end with both hands, spacing them slightly farther apart than the length of the individual fibers in the preparation. Pull gently on the sliver or roving just until you feel the fibers move past one another a little but not so far that the preparation parts completely. Move your hands down the length of sliv-

Extend the top or sliver to aerate the fibers and make them easier to draft.

er about a fiber's length and repeat the procedure. After you have extended the entire piece, that section will be longer than it was when you started, lively, fluffy, and easy to spin.

QUICK REFERENCE GUIDE FOR FLEECE PREPARATION

This guide brings together the important features of the different preparation methods so that you may compare them. The column headings represent the factors to consider when deciding on a preparation method for a particular project. The following brief discussion of the likely effect of these factors on your yarn may help you come to a decision.

Fiber arrangement contributes to the smoothness of the yarn. Parallel arrangements lead to smooth, lustrous, even yarns that highlight lustrous fleece. Nonparallel preparations make yarns that are lighter, fluffier, and hold more trapped air (and therefore, are warmer).

Fiber length also affects smoothness. Preparation methods that remove the shortest fibers, leaving only the long, usually result in smoother, more lustrous, and stronger yarn.

Waste depends on the quality of the fleece and the preparation method. Only you can determine whether the amount of waste is acceptable in terms of your fleece, the yarn, and the project. For instance, combing a fleece that has hay in it may produce substantial waste while leaving you with a small amount of a superior spinning preparation; however, this may be preferable to a large quantity of a preparation filled with chaff.

Blending allows you to turn a good-qual

QUICK REFERENCE GUIDE TO FLEECE PREPARATION METHODS

Method	Fiber arrangement	Fiber length	Waste	Blending	Equipment needed	Fleece Qualities	Yarn types
Flick-carding	Parallel	Long and short	Low to moderate	No	Flick carder and leather, vinyl, or canvas cloth	Consistent quality, medium to long staple	Smooth yarns with moderate loft
Single comb	Parallel	Long	Moderate to high	No	Dog comb, flick carder, or hackle	Consistent quality, medium to long staple	Suitable for worsted spinning; smooth lustrous yarns
Wool combs	Parallel	Long	High	Yes, if fibers are similar length	Pair of wool combs and diz	Long to medium/short staple, sound fleeces	Suitable for worsted spinning; smooth, lustrous, even yarns
Drum-carding	Parallel or non-parallel	Long and short	Low	Yes	Drum carder and doffer	All fleeces, including those of inconsistent character	Even yarns with moderate loft and luster
Hand-carding	Parallel or non-parallel	Long and short	Low	Yes	Pair of hand cards	Short to medium/long staple	Suitable for woollen spinning; soft, light yarn with maximum bulk and least weight
Picking and teasing	Non-parallel	Long and short	Low	Yes	Picker or hands	All sound fleeces and types including those of inconsistent character	Soft, light yarns with texture; may be used as preparation for other methods
Commercial combed preparation (top)	Parallel	Long	Very low	Yes	None	All sound fleeces; check with carding company for very fine	Suitable for worsted spinning; smooth, lustrous, even yarns
Commercial carded preparation (sliver)	Non-parallel	Long and short	Very low	Yes	None	All fleeces; check with carding company for very fine	Light, soft yarns, often textured

ity but inconsistent fleece into a consistent yarn. Blending is also an invaluable technique for creating special effects produced by combining two or more types of fleece, mixing wool with other fibers, or intermingling colors.

The *equipment needed* for each preparation method may vary from very simple and readily available tools to complex and expensive machines. When you are considering the use of unfamiliar equipment, rely on the manufacturer's instructions when available and read about the experiences and recommendations of other spinners or talk with them in person. It may be possible—and economical—to rent special-purpose equipment from your guild or from a local fiber store.

Fleece qualities affect preparation methods. You can prepare almost any fleece by any method, but the qualities listed are those that we believe necessary to give you consistently manageable results for a reasonable investment of time in any particular method.

Types of yarn are not limited by the fleece you start with, but the preparation method will always influence your results. This section notes the types of yarns or yarn properties that are most likely to be produced

The same Corriedale fleece prepared five different ways will produce five subtly different yarns. Clockwise from upper left: drum-carded batt, hand-teased locks, flick-carded locks, combed top, and hand-carded rolags.

202

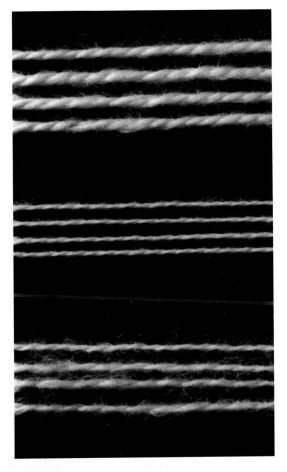

Drum-carded English Leicester fleece spun with a short draw for smoothness and to enhance luster.

English Leicester fleece combed with paddle combs and spun with a short draw for smoothness and strength.

English Leicester flick-carded then teased by hand and spun without any tension in the drafting zone to preserve the air trapped between the fibers.

by each method.

DRAFTING

The drafting technique that we describe here is only one of many, but it is one that we have found to be most useful and versatile. It can be used for a long or short draw, is the least likely to produce lumps and bumps (unless you *choose* to introduce them), and can be used to produce quantities of yarn with speed. The twist at the base of the drafting triangle almost automatically sustains the number of fibers within a yarn.

Many of you will be familiar with this technique. We suggest that those of you who haven't yet, give it a try—your efforts will be well rewarded. If you are accustomed to pushing your fiber toward the orifice, you may need a little practice before you feel entirely comfortable drafting away from the orifice.

First, be sure you are sitting in a comfortable chair, and that your hands, with arms bent at right angles at the elbows, are more or less in line with the orifice. This applies to any spinning method. Bodies, spinning wheels, and chairs all come in different shapes and sizes, and they don't all go together well! It is important for enjoyable, ache-free spinning that your body be correctly aligned.

Set up your wheel with a bobbin and thread the leader through the orifice in the usual manner. Hold the fiber to be spun in the hand that feels most comfortable. Many right-handed people hold their fiber in the left hand. It doesn't matter which hand you hold it in; it does matter that it is comfortable for you. Adjust the tension for moderate take-up and attach the fibers to the bobbin leader. *Hint:* Tying a loop on the end of your leader provides a simple means for firmly attaching your fibers, or

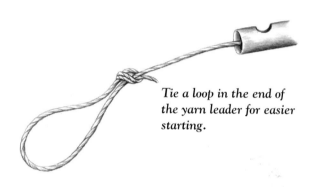

Tie a loop in the end of the yarn leader for easier starting.

your yarns if you are plying. Open the loop, just tuck a few fibers over, and off you go. No more discouraging joins or messy knots!

Use any method to spin up a yard (meter) or so of the size yarn you wish to produce. Then, keeping your hands in position, stop treadling and look at where the spun yarn meets the unspun yarn. You should see a triangle of fibers fanning out

The drafting triangle or drafting zone is the region where fibers are attenuated but not yet twisted into yarn.

from the end of the spun yarn. This is referred to as the *drafting triangle* or *drafting zone*.

1. With the thumb and forefinger of the nonfiber hand, pinch the spun yarn just above the apex of the triangle. *This is the secret to avoiding lumps.*

2. While treadling, move the fiber-supply hand away or back from the orifice to a distance slightly shorter than the length of the staple or fiber you are using.

3. Release the thumb and forefinger from the spun yarn so that the twist can run down the fibers you have drafted, and bring the fiber-supply hand forward to allow the yarn to run onto the bobbin.

Repeat steps 1, 2, and 3.

When you release the thumb and forefinger in step 3, you may use these fingers to lightly run down the yarn along with the twist. This will encourage any stray fibers to tuck themselves into the yarn. Of course, if you want hairs on the surface (for example, if you are spinning mohair), don't do this.

Notice how the spun yarn tends to draw the right amount of fiber from your fiber supply as long as it has the opportunity. As with every process in spinning, your first goal is to develop a rhythm. As you become more comfortable with drafting away from the orifice, you can adapt the technique to a long draw. Keeping the forward hand close to the orifice, draft back with the other hand, now and then lifting your forward thumb and forefinger to allow twist to travel back to the apex of the drafting triangle. Consistent twist at the apex will keep a consistent number of fibers feeding into the yarn. Very soon, you will be able to extend the draw as far back as your arm can comfortably go and can let the twist run down the fibers as they are drawn out.

When you reach this point, you may need to reposition your chair so that your elbow doesn't run into the chair back. At last we know why spinning chairs are made with tall and narrow backs!

Consistent drafting (both in length and volume of fiber) and run-on to the bobbin will produce its own rhythm *and* a yarn which has the same diameter and amount of twist from *go* to *whoa*. Perfection exists only in a perfect world, of course, but concentrate on developing a rhythm and you may be surprised to find consistent yarn easier to achieve than you had thought.

PLYING, FOLDING, OR DOUBLING

Plying is the twisting together of two or more single strands. It adds strength, bulk, and stability to a yarn, making it more versatile and easier to handle. Many of the plied yarns that we produce are *balanced* yarns, in which the twist in the singles is balanced by the reverse twist of plying and the fibers themselves lie relatively straight and approximately parallel to the axis of the yarn. If you fold a length of freshly plied balanced yarn and hold the ends together, the strands will hang parallel and not twist around one another.

If you hold a freshly spun single yarn in the same manner as you held the freshly plied yarn above, it twists itself around and then stops. Look at it carefully and you will see that the twist is in the opposite direction to that in which it was spun so that it can balance the twist in the fibers. You can

Drafting

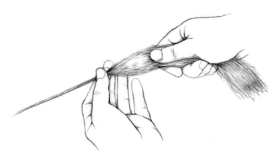

1. Pinch the yarn just above the drafting triangle.

2. Move the fiber-supply hand away.

3. Release the pinch to allow the drafted fibers to twist.

Balanced yarn.

use this test on a freshly spun single to determine how much twist to put in when plying to make a balanced yarn.

Hint: If your single has been sitting on the bobbins for any length of time, the twist will already have started to set. Using the above test on a partly set yarn will give you misleading information as to how much plying twist to add, and you will probably end up with an underplied yarn. However, if you fold a length of the single as many times as you plan to have plies (doubled for a two-ply, trebled for a three-ply, and so on) and quickly wash it in warm water, the washing will undo the setting, and the yarns will twist together into a balanced yarn. You can then measure how many twists per inch you will need to achieve that balance. In general, the twist in the plied yarn is about one-half that in the singles, regardless of the number of plies.

When aiming for an even plied yarn, it is important to keep equal tension on all the strands as they twist together. The strands are more easily controlled if they are kept separated. The fingers of the drafting hand make good separators, or you may use a plying template, which is a disk with holes and thread each strand through a separate hole.

The plastic disks from the tops of some spice jars may be used if the holes are big enough to allow your singles to slide smoothly through, or you can simply punch smooth holes in a firm piece of plastic or cardboard.

Spinners everywhere have a variety of effective methods for plying. Rhythm is the key as it is in spinning. In plying as in spinning, put the same amount of twist into the same length of yarn and your finished product will be even and pleasing.

Many spinning wheels have provision for bobbin storage built into the base unit. This is often described as a "built-in lazy kate". Certainly you can ply with the bobbins in these storage positions, but the yarn has to make an abrupt change in direction to get from the bobbins to your hands and then to the flyer. This makes for a jerky runoff from the bobbins and lessens the control you have over the rate of take-up. A cheap and convenient, freestanding lazy kate can be made from a shoebox or other similar sized box with knitting needles poked through the sides to hold the bobbins. Overwind may be controlled by securing small pieces of foam rubber to the

Plying template.

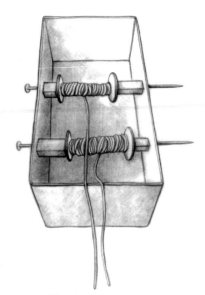

Shoebox lazy kate.

knitting needle to completely fill the spaces between each end of the bobbin and the side of the box.

Place the lazy kate in a position that will allow the yarn a straight, smooth runoff from the bobbins to the orifice. You may find it more comfortable to have the lazy kate raised about 12 inches (30 cm) from the floor and placed slightly behind your body. For some spinners, positioning the lazy kate well behind the body works best. (If you use a ladder-style lazy kate and are making a two-ply yarn, use the bottom rungs of the ladder for greater stability.) Experiment to find the most satisfactory position for you. Thread the leader through the orifice first, tie the ends of the singles to the leader on a fresh bobbin on the flyer, or place them through a loop on the leader (see page 204). Have a sample that you made by folding your singles (see page 205) handy for comparison with your plied yarn.

If you are using a wheel with Scotch tension, adjust the tension on the brake band so that it will permit immediate take-up to the bobbin as soon as you release pressure on the yarn. This will be a little greater than the tension which you would normally use for spinning singles.

Place the hand farthest from the orifice in a comfortable position on your knee, where it will remain until you've finished plying. Because the distance between your fixed hand and the orifice does not vary, that solves the problem of constant length. You'll be able to maintain a constant length in the sections of yarn being plied.

Now to determine a constant twist rate. Depressing the treadle the same number of times for each similar length of yarn should produce a steady twist rate over the entire length of the yarns being plied.

Separate the yarns with your fingers (or

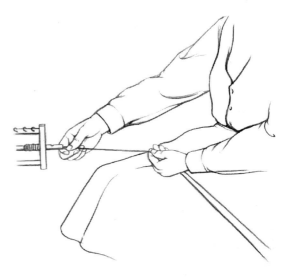

The distance between the orifice and the anchored rear hand represents a constant length.

a template) so that any snarls or pigtails will be smoothed out as they slip through. Depress the treadle twice, holding the yarns firmly in the fixed hand so that they do not draw onto the bobbin. Stop and look at the results. Is there sufficient twist to make a satisfactory yarn? The answer will probably be "no" at this stage.

Give the treadle another press and have another look. Keep adding one beat of the treadle at a time, until the yarn matches your balanced sample. Then feed the entire measured length onto the bobbin with one beat of the treadle, using the moving hand to control the yarn's movement. The fixed hand stays exactly where it is and only relaxes its grip on the yarns so they can feed onto the bobbin.

You will now have a new length of unplied yarn, exactly the same length as before, between the orifice and your fixed hand. Because you counted the beats of the treadle required to give you the amount of twist you want, you know exactly how many times to press the treadle for each similar length, and you can continue plying evenly.

After about four lengths have been twisted together, check the yarn on the bobbin to confirm that it still looks like your sample. If not, adjust the number of beats per length accordingly. Use fewer beats if there seems to be too much twist or more if there is not enough.

Run the moving hand gently down the yarn behind the twist as you are treadling, counting as you go. This will help get the rhythm established and smooth any loose hairs into the yarn. If you particularly want a hairy or fluffy yarn, omit the smoothing.

There will, of course, be a few inconsistencies, especially when you encounter a lump, bump, or thin spot in the singles, but generally speaking, the twist in the plied yarn will be consistent over the entire length.

If you are using a double band wheel, the same principles apply in general. The big difference is that it is not always easy to get the instant wind-on with this type of wheel. When determining the number of beats of the treadle to a length of yarn, therefore, you also need to take into account the number of beats needed to get the yarn onto the bobbin. When you've established your formula to your satisfaction, proceed with plying in the same way as given for the Scotch-tension wheel.

PLYING VARIATIONS

Various methods of manipulating the yarn during plying give different results or effects. If you hold yarns being plied with unequal tension, then the one yarn held with less tension may wrap around the other. This can be a useful technique for making designer yarns, but for a standard yarn it is usually undesirable.

You can do anything at all if it achieves the result that you require. The point is that you do it because you choose to do it, not because it just happens. So often, you will hear a spinner say, "but my wheel won't do that!" The occasions on which this statement is true are few. Unless there is some limitation in the design of the wheel (such as ratios too small to comfortably produce a good, soft bulky yarn or too large to handle a very fine yarn satisfactorily), the spinner is (or should be) in control of the tool.

You are the master, and with knowledge, understanding, and experience will be able to get from the wheel what you require. Don't be bullied by your wheel. Give it the right messages, and it will respond just like the family dog or (in the case of some family dogs we know) even better!

NAVAJO-PLYING

Navajo-plying produces a yarn of several colors for occasions when you wish to retain solid color in blocks instead of ending up with the tweedy effect of plying several colors together. The finished yarn is always three-ply, triple the bulk of the base yarn. Keep this in mind when planning the diameter of your singles. You will need slightly less twist in a single for a three-ply yarn than you would for a two-ply yarn with the same handle.

Spin a singles using a series of colors or shades. Plan the length of each color to be about three times the length you would like it to be in the finished yarn. When you are ready to ply, place a filled bobbin on a lazy

Navajo-Plying

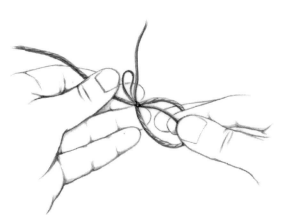

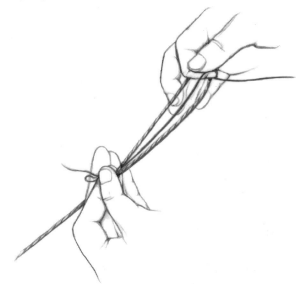

1. Holding the loop open with one hand, put the thumb and forefinger of the other hand down through the loop and pick up the single lying below.

2. Draw the single back up through the loop as far as you can reasonably manage.

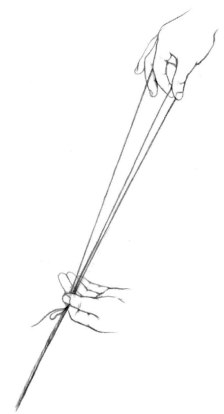

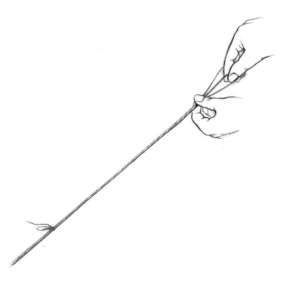

3. Reach through the new loop, grab and hold the free-hanging single without pulling it through.

4. Slide the forward hand away from the orifice to with in a few inches of the junction of the three strands. Treadle to allow the twist to run down the yarn, trying to keep even tension on all three strands as the twist runs into them.

kate and a new bobbin on the flyer spindle. Tie the end of the single to the leader with a large loop.

Use the largest whorl available and treadle *very slowly*. If you have ever crocheted a chain, the process will seem familiar: you will finger-crochet large loops and let the twist join them together.

1. Holding the loop open with one hand, put the thumb and forefinger of the other hand down through the loop and pick up the single lying below.

2. Draw the single back up through the loop as far as you can reasonably manage. You will now have a new loop.

3. Reach through the new loop, grab and hold the free-hanging single without pulling it through.

4. Slide the forward hand away from the orifice to within a few inches of the junction of the three strands (this is to allow space for your next draw-through). Treadling will allow the twist to run down the yarn. Try to keep even tension on all three strands as the twist runs into them.

5. Let the yarn run onto the bobbin.

Repeat steps 2 through 5.

Don't be discouraged by the length of the directions. This technique is much easier than it sounds and is really fun to do. An added advantage is that instead of winding off all those ends that seem to collect on bobbins and putting them into a basket or just throwing them away, you can instead Navajo-ply them off the bobbin and have some useful sample yarns. This is the technique used to make the yarn for the Jacob fleece sample on page 163.

FINISHING TECHNIQUES FOR FIBER, YARN, AND FABRIC

WASHING FLEECE

There are as many different recipes for washing fleece as there are people who wash it. If your method gives you the results you require, then go ahead and use it. You may, however, find it helpful to examine what goes on during washing and then determine whether your current method gives you the best possible results.

Washing removes grease, suint, dirt and dust, and loose vegetation from the wool.

Each fiber is coated with a layer of wool wax or grease. Most wool grease melts at between 110° and 120°F (43° and 49°C), so if your washing liquid is cooler, the grease will not be removed. Grease can cause problems when the yarn is woven or knitted into cloth or garments. In the skein, it may not be noticed, but when the yarn is worked up, natural white fleece can appear yellowed and patchy. Residual grease can also contribute to uneven dyeing.

Suint, or sweat, is cold water-soluble. Dirt and dust can be much more effectively removed in hot water.

Having prepared a basin of water at a suitable temperature, it is time to add the washing agent. For years, pure soap flakes were considered the ideal cleanser for wool. This was before the development of detergents and also before the introduction of special wool-washing detergents. Ah, you may say, just more manufacturer's hype! But wait a minute:

♦ Wool can be harmed by alkaline solutions, and soap is an alkaline substance.

- Detergents contain wetting agents, which will ensure that the wool is thoroughly wet.
- High-quality wool detergents have a pH level which falls within the safest range for wool.
- Detergents will also prevent the appearance of brownish stains caused by high levels of iron oxide, which is present in some natural water supplies.

Washing soda is sometimes suggested as a good means of removing grease from wool. Although it is effective, it is alkaline and likely to cause yellowing. We don't recommend it.

Two washings with warm water and plenty of washing agent are recommended and are usually sufficient.

Rinsing is also a vital part of successful cleansing. Rinse water needs to be at the same temperature as the washing water to ensure that the grease will be rinsed out and not redeposited on the fiber. A number of wool-wash products are promoted as requiring "no rinsing"; however, rinsing removes any remaining dirt and reduces any remaining alkalinity. Again, we recommend two rinses.

SETTING TWIST

Setting twist is a means of controlling the curling, twisting, and snarling of singles or unbalanced plied yarns so that they will be easier to handle. In the simplest form of setting twist, wool fibers are wetted thoroughly and then dried under tension just like setting human hair. Yarn set this way will remain set only until it is immersed in water again, allowing the fibers to return to their original shape. Even high atmospheric humidity can be enough to unset yarn. Setting a yarn under tension also straightens some of the crimp in the wool fiber and consequently removes some of the loft and elasticity of a yarn; however, these qualities also return when the setting process is reversed.

Setting can be made more permanent by exposing the yarn to heat as well as moisture. Under these conditions, the wool fibers become pliable and can be reshaped. The reshaping or setting normally lasts until the wool is subjected to a higher temperature than that which was used for the original shaping. Truly permanent setting can only be accomplished either by rearranging the structure of the wool fiber in a chemical process (very much like a permanent wave) or by setting the yarn with steam at a temperature of 248°F (120°C).

Setting should be carried out only when there is a clear reason for doing so. Balanced plied yarns seldom need more than a warm-water wash (see page 212), but a singles yarn for weaving will probably be much easier to manage if it has been dried under tension. To choose the most appropriate method for setting twist, consider how much twist you want to control, how much loft and elasticity you want to retain, and whether the setting should be permanent or should last just during construction of the fabric or garment. To prevent damage and possible loss of strength, loft, or character, handle yarns gently when they are wet or hot, and never overstretch them. The following four methods vary in the amount of twist that can be controlled and the permanence of the set.

Leaving yarn on the bobbin. Yarn left wound on a bobbin under tension will gradually become set. A few days will usually make a soft twist easier to handle; more complete setting may take weeks or

Method	Equipment	Reversed by	Special characteristics	Suitable for the following yarns
Sitting on bobbin	None	Immersion in water or high humidity	Degree of set varies by length of time yarn is left	Soft twist singles
Warm water wash	None	Immersion in water or high humidity	Preserves maximum loft and elasticity	Balanced, plied yarns for knitting or weaving
Warm water wash and extension	Weights or yarn blocker	Immersion in water or high humidity	Partial loss of loft and elasticity reversed by immersion in water	Designer yarns with mixed plies and soft to medium twist singles or unbalanced plied yarns
Steaming	Steamer or large pot and steam resistant reel or niddy noddy	Steaming at similar or higher temperature	Permanently changes structure of the wool fibers	High-twist singles or unbalanced yarns, especially for weaving. Singles spun from strong fleeces

months. This can be a good choice if you plan to take the yarn directly from spinning wheel to loom and then wash and finish the fabric after it is off the loom.

Warm-water wash. Washing is an essential part of finishing most wool yarns. It allows the fibers to relax and regain their original shape after being under tension during spinning. The true character of your yarn will emerge only after it has been washed. Use a small quantity of detergent and warm or hot water to remove the last traces of dirt and oil from the fibers. Rinse well. If the yarn is balanced or close to balanced, you probably won't need to dry it under tension, but can allow the natural bounce and elasticity of the fleece to develop fully. Most knitting yarns benefit from this kind of finishing because it preserves loft.

Warm-water wash with extension. A skein that is washed and then dried under enough tension to straighten but not stretch the yarn will be set as it dries. Tension can be carefully applied by hanging weights on the skein or by winding the wet yarn onto a yarn blocker. If you use just enough tension to straighten the skein and no more, you will preserve as much loft and elasticity as possible. This is the method we use most often for weaving singles and for designer yarns, which may have some residual twist because of their complex construction.

Hint: If a yarn is left under tension until it is completely dry, it often appears flat and lifeless. If you remove the weights or tension just before it is totally dry, the yarn will retain some of its bounce while the twist remains set.

Steaming. Moisture and the high temperature of steam make wool fibers plastic and enable us to impose permanent structural change. Steam applied externally with a steaming kettle or hand-held steamer is most likely only to moisten the yarn and has the same effect as a warm-water wash with extension. Try this method when you wish to set twist but don't want to immerse the yarn in water.

For true steaming, you can place the yarn on a rack inside a large covered pot or steamer. The yarn must be extended and under tension during the steaming and while it cools. (See hint under warm-water wash with extension.) True steam-setting changes the structure of the wool fiber.

BLOCKING

After your wool fabric has been completed and taken off the loom or needles, it may require further finishing before it is ready for use. At least wash it if it is intended to be washable. As with yarn, washing the fabric relaxes the fibers and allows them to regain their natural shape. Wool fabrics will usually become softer and loftier, and will shrink slightly as the fibers and yarns take up.

Blocking sets the fabric by drying it under tension in the desired shape. This step is useful for extending lace to show its intricacy or for making the parts of a sweater easier to piece together.

You will need a firm surface that can accept pins and wet fabrics without damage and without staining the fabric. A cork-covered bulletin board or padded ironing board is ideal for small pieces, and towel-covered, well-anchored carpeting works well for larger ones.

To ensure that the finished shape of the fabric is correct and balanced, score the shape you want on a piece of waxed paper and place it under the piece to use as a guide while blocking. A long ruler and T square are useful for aligning large rectangular pieces.

Remove the excess moisture by rolling the wet fabric in a towel. Place the damp fabric on the surface and begin anchoring it with *rustproof* pins. Start with major landmarks, such as corners or stripes, and then pin the edges between, aiming to keep the rows, or the warp and weft threads, evenly distributed over the entire fabric. For three-dimensional pieces such as lace caps and booties, you may need to build up special forms to support the finished fabric while it is being blocked.

This form of blocking will last only until the piece is washed next or until the humidity in the air gradually releases the set. By subjecting the fabric to hot steam, you can achieve a firmer set.

Pin the piece out in the same manner, but insert the pins so that they lie flat. With the steam iron set to wool, hold it as close as possible without actually placing it on the fabric. Move the iron so that steam reaches all parts of the fabric. Leave the cloth pinned until it is completely dry. This method sets knitted, crocheted, or delicate woven fabrics without squeezing the life out of them.

Most firmly woven fabrics, particularly yardage, need steam-pressing. Use a damp press cloth between the iron and the fabric to provide extra steam and protect the fabric from scorching. Press firmly.

TAKE TIME TO UNWIND

The following exercises, selected by Beverley Harrison, a physiotherapist, weaver, and spinner and Marea Page, an occupational therapist with a Diploma of Handwoven Textiles, will help alleviate the stresses and strains of spinning, knitting, crocheting, and weaving. They are intended for persons of average fitness. If you suffer from joint pain, leave out any exercise or movement that increases the pain and ask your physical or occupational therapist for advice on how to achieve the same result in another manner.

All exercises are preferably done while standing, but if your balance is poor, you may do all except the walk-around exercise from a sitting position.

SHOULDERS

1. (a) Stand up and walk around—check the mailbox, water the houseplants, or put the kettle on.

(b) Stretch both arms above your head four to five times.

(c) Breathe in deeply through your nose, then out through your mouth, three times. (Too many deep breaths could make you feel dizzy.)

(d) Place your palms across the small of your back and arch your spine backward. Hold for 10 seconds, then relax. Repeat five times.

2. Lift your shoulders up toward your ears, then relax. Bring your shoulders forward, then relax. Move your shoulders backward, then relax. Repeat this sequence five to ten times.

3. Hold one arm above your head and push your fingers toward the ceiling. Repeat with the other arm. Continue, alternating arms, five to ten times.

4. Put your hands behind your neck, touching your fingertips together, then bring them forward. Bring your hands behind your waist, touch them together, then slide them up and back toward your shoulder blades. Continue, alternating hands behind neck and hands behind waist, five to ten times.

Finish this group of exercises by relaxing your arms by your sides and swinging them gently.

HEAD AND NECK

1. With eyes looking straight ahead, tuck your chin in to lengthen your neck as if your head is being pulled upward by a string. Hold for 10 seconds, then relax. Repeat this stretch five to ten times.

2. Turn your head to look over first one shoulder, then the other. Repeat this five to ten times in each direction.

3. Tilt your head, first moving your right ear toward your right shoulder and then your left ear toward your left shoulder. Repeat this five to ten times in each direction.

HANDS AND ARMS

1. With your arms held out in front, spread your fingers wide open, then close them to make a fist. Repeat five to ten times.

2. With your arms at your sides, rotate your hands from your wrists. Repeat circles ten times in each direction.

3. With your arms by your sides, shake your hands loosely for 15 to 30 seconds.

EYES

1. Open your eyes wide (that surprised look), then close them tight. Repeat 5–10 times.

2. Start with your eyes straight ahead. Turn them first to one side, then to the other, then up and down; do this slowly, so you won't feel dizzy. Repeat sequence five to ten times.

3. Focus on a distant object, then focus on a near object. Relax your eyes. Repeat five to ten times.

LEGS

1. Standing comfortably with your feet apart and holding onto a doorjamb for balance:

(a) Stand on your toes by lifting your heels off the floor.

(b) Stand on your heels by lifting your toes off the floor (this isn't as easy as *a*!).

2. Standing on one leg, lift the other one forward about 6 inches (15 cm) off the ground (you may need to support yourself against a table). With the lifted leg, rotate your foot at the ankle first in one direction, then the other five times. Repeat with the other leg.

POSTURE AND RELAXATION

1. Try to be aware of good posture positions at all times.

(a) Stand tall, pull your tummy in, tighten your seat, shrink around the waist, and tuck your chin in. Feel your spine lengthen.

(b) Relax your shoulders. Take some deep breaths in and out.

(c) Sit and relax and breathe quietly for a few moments.

That cup of tea will be well brewed now!

GLOSSARY

batt. Thick, airy sheet of carded fibers.

blending. Combining two or more wools or fibers together so that they behave as one.

blocking. Setting wool fabric either by stretching wet fabric into shape and allowing it to dry or by stretching the fabric into shape and heating it with steam.

break. A weakness in one portion of the staple due to thinning of the wool fibers. Associated with lower feed intake.

Bradford count (also spinning count, count, or quality number). A system of measuring the fineness of wools based on the maximum number of skeins, each 560 yards long, that can be spun from one pound of combed top. The higher the number, the finer the fleece.

bright. Description of the reflection of light from fine-wool fleeces. While the reflection is intense, it is not lustrous as in longwools. Like the reflection from sugar.

britch (also brotch or breech). The rear portion of the sheep—hind legs and buttocks.

butt end. The end of the wool staple that has been cut or shorn from the sheep.

canary stain. An unscourable yellow stain.

carding. A method of separating and aligning fibers in preparation for spinning that uses hand cards or a mechanical carder. Carding does not eliminate any fibers from the preparation but blends them together.

carding cloth. Heavy fabric or leather attached to hand carders and drum carders into which wire teeth are anchored.

carding surface. The surface created by the tips of the wire teeth of hand carders or a carding drum.

combing. Preparing fiber for spinning by removing all the foreign matter and shorter fibers, and arranging the remaining long fibers parallel to one another.

chalky. Flat and without luster. Like the light reflected from household flour.

charging. Loading hand carders with fleece ready for carding.

cortex. Long spindle-shaped cells which form the major part of the wool fiber.

cotted wool. Partially felted or matted wool which occurs while the fleece is still on the sheep.

crimp. The visible waviness in wool fibers.

crisp. The handle of wool that is somewhat stiff, but very springy.

cuticle. The outer layer of the wool fiber.

DFE (Differential friction effect). Term used to describe the one-way movement of wool fibers.

diz. A thin disc or oval of wood, bone, horn, plastic, or cardboard with a small hole through which combed fiber is drawn to form a top.

doffing rod. A long, usually steel rod used to part a drum-carded batt so that it can be removed from the drum.

double carders. Hand carders used as a pair to separate and align fibers in preparation for spinning.

drafting. The process of attenuating fibers and allowing them to twist into yarn.

drafting triangle (also drafting zone). The area where fibers are attenuated just prior to or just as they are being twisted into yarn.

drum carder. A mechanical carder which uses a system of variable diameter drums covered with carding cloth to separate and straighten the wool fibers.

dual-purpose breed. A breed that provides both meat and wool.

elasticity. The ability of a fiber to return to its original length after being stretched.

English combs. Wool combs with several rows of long pointed tines embedded in a compact wooden head with a handle. They are used as a pair.

felt. A dense wool fabric formed of tangled wool fibers. Under conditions of heat, moisture, and movement, differential friction effect (DFE) causes the wool fibers to become irreversibly interlocked.

flannel. A napped fabric woven from woolen-spun yarn.

flick carder. A small single handcarder used to separate the fibers of a lock or staple of wool in preparation for spinning without disturbing the alignment of the fibers within the lock.

follicle. An opening in the skin from which a fiber grows.

fulling. Finishing processes for woven fabrics that use DFE to meld and blend the fibers and yarns into a thicker, more cohesive fabric.

hair. Long coarse fibers intermediate between true wool and kemp. They grow continuously and do not shed like kemp. For example, the hair fibers of Drysdale or Scottish Blackface.

handle or hand. The feel of wool as assessed by touch or handling.

hogget (also hog or hogg). A young sheep of either sex approximately 9 to 18 months old.

hygroscopic. Absorbs water readily.

kemp. Short, coarse medullated fiber found in some fleeces. Usually found lying shed in the fleece. These fibers appear not to take dyes.

keratin. The protein substance which makes up the wool fiber.

lock. A natural grouping of adjacent wool fibers that occurs as the fleece grows on the sheep.

loft (also bulk). Airiness.

long draw. A method of spinning wool that combines attenuation and twisting of the fibers into yarn at the same time.

luster. The sheen caused by light reflected from the cuticle of the wool fiber.

medulla. A wool fiber's inner core, consisting of latticed cells. Usually absent in fine wools.

medullated. Wool fiber containing a core of medulla cells.

micron. 1 millionth of a meter or 1 thousandth of a millimeter. 1/25,400 (0.00004) inch.

mountain and hill breeds. A category of British sheep developed to thrive in the harsh weather conditions of the British highlands. In contrast to the sheep of the lowlands or down counties.

mushy wool. Lacking character and badly weathered.

Navajo-plying. A method of creating a three-ply yarn from a single strand. Navajo-plying preserves the distinct colors of a single yarn spun from space-dyed fiber.

neps. Clumps of short fibers that occur in prepared fiber after carding.

noils. Short and broken fibers remaining after combing. (Can often be used as a component of designer yarns.)

pH scale. A scale for measuring acidity or alkalinity of a solution. 7 is neutral. A pH below 7 is acidic and pH above 7 is alkaline. The further from 7 the pH is, the more acidic or alkaline the solution.

paddle combs. Wool combs with one or two rows of pointed tines embedded in a broad paddle-shaped wooden head attached to a handle. They are used as a pair to comb wool for spinning.

picking. Opening and teasing apart locks of wool either in preparation for spinning or as a preliminary to further preparation.

pills. Small balls of tangled fiber on the surface of a fabric.

plying (also folding or doubling). Twisting two or more single strands together.

plying template. A flat piece of wood, cardboard, or plastic with holes through which single yarns are threaded so that they may be controlled as they are plied together.

poll. Top of the sheep's head.

polled. Without horns.

relaxation shrinkage (also take-up). Wool fibers and yarns returning to their natural shape after the tensions of spinning and processing are removed.

resilience. The ability of wool to bounce back to its original bulk after being compressed.

rolag. A non-parallel preparation of fibers prepared on hand cards. The carded fibers are rolled to form a sausage-shaped bundle.

roving. A continuous strand of carded or combed fiber that has been further extended and slightly twisted.

scouring. The thorough removal of dirt and grease from wool.

semi-worsted yarn. A yarn handspun from any fiber preparation, except carded rolags, that includes both long and short fibers.

setting twist. A means of controlling the curling and twisting of unbalanced yarns so that they are easier to handle.

shorn hogget (fleece). A fleece from a sheep between the ages of seven and eighteen months that was shorn once before as a lamb.

short draw. A method for spinning yarn that attenuates the fibers before twisting them to form yarn.

shortwool. British wools with a short staple length. Usually Down-type, lowland sheep.

sliver. A continuous strand of carded fiber.

spinning count (also Bradford count, quality number). A means of describing the fineness of wool. The maximum number of skeins, each 560 yards in length, that can be spun from one pound of combed top. The higher the number, the finer the fleece.

spongy. Full handling. Able to bounce back after being squeezed.

staple. A group of wool fibers in their natural formation.

staple definition. The distinctness of the staples of locks in the fleece.

strong. A term used to describe coarse wool.

suint. Sheep perspiration.

Superwash. Wool that meets or exceeds the shrink-resistant standards established by the International Wool Secretariat.

take-up shrinkage (also relaxation shrinkage). Wool fibers and yarns returning to their natural shape after the tensions of spinning and processing are removed.

teasing. Opening the wool staple and separating the fibers.

tender. A weak point in a wool staple.

thrifty. A sheep that does well on little feed or poorer pastures.

tip. The outermost part of the wool staple.

tippy. Excessive staple tip.

top. A continuous strand of combed fiber.

topknot or wig. Wool growing on the poll.

tweed. A cloth woven from woolen-spun singles.

unscourable. Cannot be removed by thorough washing.

Viking combs. Hand-held wool combs used as a pair to comb wool for spinning. Each comb consists of one or two rows of long pointed tines embedded in a narrow wooden head attached to a handle.

washing soda. Sodium carbonate. Alkaline substance sometimes used to wash greasy fleece.

wetted. Thorough penetration of liquid.

wool carders. Hand carders used as a pair to separate and align wool fibers in preparation for spinning. The teeth of wool carders are usually coarser and spaced further apart than the teeth of fine carders which are designed for cotton, silk, and other finer fibers.

wool combs. Tools consisting of long metal tines embedded in a wooden head attached to a handle. They are used in pairs to remove foreign matter and shorter fibers and align the remaining long wool fibers parallel to one another.

wool faults. Properties of a fleece that detract from its quality or usefulness.

wool quality numbers (also Bradford count, spinning count). A means of describing the fineness of wool. The maximum number of skeins, each 560 yards in length, that can be spun from one pound of combed top. The higher the number, the finer the fleece.

woolclassing. Sorting and grading of wool into like qualities.

woolen yarn. A yarn spun from short, carded fibers.

woolly hogget (fleece). The fleece from a sheep between the ages of seven and eighteen months that has never been shorn before. A woolly hogget fleece often has characteristic corkscrew tips which are the remnants of the birth coat.

worsted yarn. A yarn spun from fibers which have been combed to remove all the shorter fibers.

yield. The proportion of clean, washed wool recovered from greasy fleece. Varies between breeds and wool types.

yolk. Combination of wax and sweat (suint) secretions that surround the wool fiber.

BIBLIOGRAPHY

American Wool Council. *Wool Grades and the Sheep that Grow the Wool*. A division of The American Sheep Producers Council, Inc.

Cook, J. Gordon. *Handbook of Textile Fibres. Vol.1 Natural Fibers*. England: Merrow Publishing Co, 1984.

Cottle, D. J.(Editor). *Australian Sheep and Wool Handbook*. Melbourne, Australia: Inkata Press, 1991.

Elliot, J., Lord, D. E., and Williams, J. M. (Eds.). *British Sheep & Wool*. Bradford, England: The British Wool Marketing Board, 1990.

Ensminger, M. E. *Sheep and Wool Science*. Danville, IL: Interstate, 1970.

Harmsworth, T. and Day, G. *Wool and Mohair. 2nd Ed*. Victoria, Australia: Inkata Press, 1990.

Henderson, A. E. *Wool and Woolclassing*. Wellington, New Zealand: A. H. and A. W. Reed, 1965.

Henderson, A. E. *Growing Better Wool*. Wellington, New Zealand: A. H. and A. W. Reed, 1968.

Hochberg, Bette. *Fibre Facts*. Santa Cruz, CA: Bette Hochberg, 1981.

Horn, Beverly. *Fleece in Your Hands, Revised Edition*. Loveland, Colorado: Interweave Press, 1979.

Jackson, Constance and Plowman, Judith. *The Woolcraft Book*. Auckland, New Zealand: Collins, 1980.

Jefferies, B. C. *New Sheep Breeds of Australia*. In *Colored Sheep and Wool: Exploring Their Beauty and Function*. The Proceedings of the World Congress on Colored Sheep U. S. A. 1989. Edited by Erskine, Kent. Ashland, OR: Black Sheep Press, 1989.

Leeder, John. D. *Wool–Nature's Wonder Fibre*. Victoria, Australia: Australasian Textiles Publishers, 1984.

Mason, I. L. *A World Dictionary of Livestock Breeds Types and Varieties*. Wallinford, U.K.: C.A.B. International, 1988.

McKinney, J. *The Sheep Book*. New York: Wiley, 1959.

New Zealand Wool Board. *New Zealand Sheep and Their Wool*. New Zealand: New Zealand Wool Board, 1983.

Ponting, Kenneth G. *Sheep of the World*. Poole: Blandford Press, 1980.

Ross, Mabel. *The Encyclopedia of Hand Spinning*. Loveland, CO: Interweave Press, 1988.

Ryder, M. L. *Sheep and Man*. London: Duckworth, 1983.

Ryder, M. L. and Stephenson, S. K. *Wool Growth*. London: Academic Press, 1968.

Sponenberg, D. P. *Comparative Pigmentation of Sheep, Goats, and Llamas—What Colors are Possible Through Selection*. In *Colored Sheep and Wool: Exploring Their Beauty and Function*. The Proceedings of the World Congress on Colored Sheep U. S. A. 1989. Edited by Erskine, Kent. Ashland, OR: Black Sheep Press, 1989.

Starmore, Alice. *Alice Starmore's Book of Fair Isle Knitting*. Newtown, CT: Taunton Press, 1988.

Stove, Margaret. *Handspinning Dyeing and Working with Merino and Superfine Wools in New Zealand*. Christchurch, New Zealand: The Caxton Press, 1991.

Teal, Peter. *Hand Woolcombing and Spinning*. Wellington, New Zealand: A. H. and A. W. Reed, 1977.

Von Bergen, Werner and Mauersberger, Herbert R. *American Wool Handbook, 2nd Edition*. New York: Textile Book Publishers, 1948.

INDEX